"Today it is no longer fashionable to ~~a~~
methods. However, in order to achieve ~~b~~
mander must exhibit extraordinarily high s
ment as he exhorts his troops in an enterpr..
supreme sacrifice of death. The good general rejects the crude weapons of coercion, which, it is true, are available in a military context. Instead he works through individuals and teams, combining all the best principles of forward planning, man management and initiative. These are as applicable in the field of business as they are in that of battle.

"It is not surprising therefore that Khoo Kheng-Hor goes back to one of China's most famous generals, Sun Tzu, to look for ways in which his brilliance may be aptly applied to today's business methods. As Mr Khoo says in his first edition of the book, both the art of war and the art of business are about "achieving success through people". Concentrate on that aspect of a good general's skill and you have, as Mr Khoo shows, a fascinatingly apt parallel with today's business world."

PETER R. NIGHTINGALE
Managing Director
Swire Marketing Limited

"Looking at the works of Sun Tzu in today's environment sheds a great deal of light on the currect discussion of leadership versus management. Many enterprises in the last decade have suffered or even ceased because they have been run by managers who have just offered "more of the same" albeit more efficiently. These managers have not developed a vision and strategies for the company based on customer input that will take them into the 21st century to serve the market better, faster and cheaper.

"Those companies that have been blessed with a visionary who understands not just today but has a picture of tomorrow and understands the role of all the resources of the company in this vision together with the importance of communication in the process, will be the winners.

"Sun Tzu was just such a general and his understanding of the roles of all the participants in war provides today's leaders with a very relevant set of principles for execution."

PETER ELLIS
Senior Vice President/Area General Manager
ASEAN and South Asia
American Express International, Inc.

"... Khoo has managed to bring the whole subject to a most welcomed level of realism by injecting examples of actual management situations he has come across in his career... The most notable aspect of the book however is how Khoo has managed to translate what is a complicated treatise into a easily readable and, more importantly, understandable prose. It is written in a swift and simple style that allows for both easy understanding and retention... All in all, the book is certainly worth a read, especially for people in management."

GOPAL SREENEVASAN
Book Reviewer
Malaysian Business (Nov. 1992)

SUN TZU & MANAGEMENT

by the author of War At Work:
Applying Sun Tzu's
Art of War
in today's business world

KHOO KHENG-HOR

Pelanduk
Publications

Published by
Pelanduk Publications (M) Sdn. Bhd.,
24 Jalan 20/16A, 46300 Petaling Jaya,
Selangor Darul Ehsan,
Malaysia.

All correspondence to:
Pelanduk Publications (M) Sdn. Bhd.,
P.O. Box 8265, 46785 Kelana Jaya,
Selangor Darul Ehsan, Malaysia.

1st printing July 1992
2nd printing September 1992
3rd printing May 1993
4h printing October 1993

REVISED EDITION
5th printing June 1994
6th printing April 1995
7th printing January 1996

Perpustakaan Negara Malaysia   Cataloguing-in-Publication Data

Khoo, Kheng-Hor
    Sun Tzu & Management/Khoo Kheng-Hor.
    ISBN 967-978-424-X
    1. Management. I. Title.
    658.

Printed by
Eagle Trading Sdn. Bhd.

Contents

PART II – Managing Oneself

PART III – Managing The Internal Environment

PART IV – Managing The External Environment

PART V – Conclusion

The Author

As a business executive, consultant, author and speaker, Khoo Kheng-Hor has been described as a contemporary interpreter of Sun Tzu's treatise, *Art of War*. He has been interviewed on television, radio, newspapers and magazines for his creative interpretations of Sun Tzu's war principles for use, not only in strategic management, but also in specific areas of management such as marketing, customer service and human resource management, as well as corporate politics.

He now lives in Singapore with his wife, Judy, and besides running Stirling Training & Management Consultants Pte Ltd, his own firm which assists clients in planning and implementing strategies and motivating their executives through his specially-developed "Management, the Sun Tzu Way" programs, he also writes a monthly column for *Asia-21* and *Certified Management Digest (CMD)* and lectures part-time for the Singapore Institute of Management's external degree programs.

His other books are *War at Work: Applying Sun Tzu's Art of War in Today's Business World*, *Sun Tzu's Art of War* (a translation), *Personnel Management Manual*, *Personnel Policies* and *Applying Sun Tzu's Art of War in Corporate Politics*.

Acknowledgement

I HAVE WORKED on this book for a long time and owe so much to so many people. It is however not possible to acknowledge all those who have provided me with the ideas and materials for this book. They include both former and present bosses, colleagues, staff, and associates whom I met in the course of my career; both lecturers and fellow students during my year of study at the University of Stirling, Scotland; and the participants who attended my public lectures and in-house seminars.

Tan Aik Seng, Maggie Foo, Tan Meng Kwang, Peter Khoo and wife, Madeline, Elizabeth Seah and husband, Teng Kow, Bee Hong and husband, Tao Hai Sin have all made very special contributions to the development of my work, and I am fortunate to have them as friends.

Finally, as always, I am lucky to have the support of my wife, Judy, who has contributed to this book in so many ways (e.g. for her calligraphy), and who has helped to make the writing of this book a happy and rewarding experience.

Preface

WHEN I FIRST wrote the materials which were subsequently published as *War At Work – Applying Sun Tzu's Art of War In Today's Business World*, it was my intention then to share my understanding of Sun Tzu's work with my team of managers at The Mall shopping complex and Fameland Sdn Bhd.

The interpretations were not meant to provide a sure-fire formula for success but rather to throw hints which may be useful in provoking and subsequently developing my managers to think strategically and lead by example.

When the book was published, the same hints were made available to my readers so that they too could develop their own strategies when it comes to "waging war" with their rivals in the office or in the market.

Since then, feedback has indicated that while a book like *War At Work – Applying Sun Tzu's Art of War In Today's Business World* is appreciated for the said hints in an easy-to-read format, a second book giving more textbook-type details on the application of Sun Tzu's war principles is highly desirable, especially for the more serious readers. For example, the well-known maxim coined by Mao Tse-tung, "Know yourself, know your enemy, one hundred battles, one hundred victories," which came from a partial quote from Sun Tzu's work, could be further illustrated in conjunction with a S.W.O.T. (the acronym for Strengths-Weaknesses-Opportunities-Threats) analysis.

I have also found that there is a demand for more information on how to use Sun Tzu's war principles for countering the "back-stabbers" from the same side within one's organization. On reflection, I cannot help seeing the logic behind this demand considering the countless examples of the seemingly irrational behaviors which people can display at the workplace, either over imagined slights, inherent paranoia, or simply part of the rituals of the corporate "power game". I remember witnessing at a meeting when the more the executives tried to reason with a particularly hot-headed colleague, the more violent the course of argument took.

I even recall one particular assistant general manager who, in the absence of his boss, gleefully took the opportunity to make life miserable for those managers (including junior officers) whom he imagined to have slighted him in the past, when he should be using his effort and energy for the more critical task of proving his worth in taking the reins of leadership to consolidate the company against an aggressive business competitor at the time. And of course, at some time or other, some of us may have encountered those "red-tapes" executives who take delight in insisting that all requisitions be filled in specially-designed forms in triplicates, and then promptly sitting on the forms for weeks before acting on them.

It goes without saying then that any manager seeking success must work toward controlling himself and both the internal and external environments. It is with this need in mind that this book is planned to cover five parts.

The first part seeks to provide the readers with a basic understanding of Sun Tzu's work, its application and strategic significance; the second, to look within oneself as the starting point in developing an awareness of one's strengths and weaknesses as well as highlighting the responsibility of being the boss; the third, to view the internal environment, i.e. one's immediate operating environment, with an insight into office politicking and giving suggestions on how to cope with it; the fourth, to show the relevance of Sun Tzu's works in formulating and implementing strategies in the increasingly competitive world of business and what is commonly referred to as the external environment; and the fifth, to conclude by sharing my views on how the Japanese has benefited from Sun Tzu's *Art of War* to become the leading economy today.

We, Chinese, have a saying: "If excellence can be attained, then it is probably not worth having". As such, I must add that despite the compliments and congratulations I have received from my readers and friends since this book was published about two years, I am still far from being satisfied. Indeed, no student of Sun Tzu can afford to stray into complacency ...hence, the launch of this second edition which has also seen me honing my skills as a manager (and student of Sun Tzu) since then.

Khoo Kheng-Hor

Introducing Sun Tzu and the *Art Of War*

WHAT HAS A 2,500-year-old Chinese military strategist to do with Management?

The answer: Plenty. The war principles as found in Sun Tzu's book, *Art of War*, has much in common with the present-day aim of achieving success through people in business, if one cares to relate Sun Tzu's sayings to the modern context, minus the archaic fondness for grandiose expressions.

To understand the man and his work, it is appropriate to narrate the following story which is familiar to many Chinese (and an even greater number of Japanese):

> Around 500BC when Sun Tzu, a native of Qi, wrote the *Art of War*, He Lu, the Prince of Wu, was so impressed by what he read that he granted him an audience.
>
> Prince He Lu who had read all of Sun Tzu's 13 chapters on warfare, wanted to test Sun Tzu's skill in drilling troops, using women. Sun Tzu was prepared to face this test and Prince He Lu sent for 180 ladies from his palace.
>
> Sun Tzu divided them into two companies, each headed by one of the Prince's two favorite concubines. After arming all the women with spears, Sun

Tzu asked: "Do you know what is front and back, right and left?"

When all the women replied in the affirmative, Sun Tzu went on to instruct them thus: "When I command 'front', you must face directly ahead; 'turn left', you must face to the left; 'turn right', you must face to the right; 'back', you must turn right around towards your back."

As all the women assented, Sun Tzu laid out the executioner's weapons to show his seriousness on discipline and began the drill to the sounds of drum beats and shouts of commands. None of the women moved and instead they burst into laughter.

Sun Tzu patiently told them that commands which are unclear and, therefore, not thoroughly understood would be the commander's fault, and proceeded to instruct them once more.

When the drums were beaten a second time and the commands repeated, the women again burst into fits of laughter. This time Sun Tzu said: "Commands which are unclear and not thoroughly understood would be the commander's fault. But when commands are clear and the soldiers nonetheless do not carry them out, then it is the fault of their officers". So saying, he ordered both concubines who were heading the two companies out for execution.

The Prince, who was witnessing the drill from a raised pavilion, on seeing his favorite concubines sent out for execution, was greatly alarmed and quickly sent an aide with the message: "I believe the general is capable of drilling troops. Without these two concubines, my food and drink will be tasteless. It is my desire that they be spared".

Sun Tzu replied that having received the royal commission to lead the troops in the field, he can disregard any of the Ruler's commands as he sees fit. Accordingly, he had the two concubines beheaded as an example and thereafter appointed two women next in line to replace the executed ones as Company Leaders.

Subsequently, the drill proceeded smoothly with every woman turning left, right, front, or back; kneeling or rising, with perfect accuracy and precision, without uttering any dissent.

Sun Tzu then sent a messenger to the Prince requesting him to inspect the troops which he declared as having been properly drilled and disciplined, and prepared even to go through fire and water for the Prince.

When the Prince declined, Sun Tzu remarked: "The Prince is only fond of words which he cannot put into practice".

Greatly ashamed by what he heard, and recognizing Sun Tzu's ability, Prince He Lu promptly appointed Sun Tzu as the supreme commander of the Wu armies.

In 506BC, Sun Tzu led five expeditions against the State of Chu which had regarded Wu as a vassal. He defeated the armies of Chu and forced his way into the Chu capital, Ying-du, while King Zhao fled, leaving his State on the verge of extermination.

For almost 20 years thereafter, the armies of Wu continued to be victorious against those of its neighbors, the States of Qi, Qin and Yue. However, after his death, his successors failed to follow his precepts and suffered defeat after defeat until 473BC when the kingdom became extinct.

PART I

An Overview: Applying Sun Tzu's *Art Of War* In Today's Management

PLANNING

According to Sun Tzu, "More planning shall give more chances of victory. So how about totally without planning?" One must thus be capable of planning well ahead.

CHAPTER 1

Introduction

AS THE OLDEST military treatise among the Chinese classical works, Sun Tzu's *Art of War* is surprisingly a very short book, containing only some 6,000 characters in Chinese literary writing. Compressed into 13 chapters, the longest is Chapter 11, 'The Nine Varieties Of Ground,' which contains just over 1,000 characters, while the shortest is Chapter 8, 'Tactical Variations' containing less than 250 characters. This 2,500-year-old book has however continued to provoke much interest among military leaders and businessmen even in modern times.

Although it is such a short book, there is much that we can learn from the Art of War and I have never stopped marvelling at how applicable Sun Tzu's principles are to contemporary business as they are to war. The urgency of being kept updated on the enemies' plans and movement as well as court intrigues of ancient times are no different from today's priority for management information to keep track of competitors' movement, and of course, the daily office politicking. It is just a case of history repeating itself albeit in a different ambience and setting.

Since Sun Tzu's *Art of War* is such a short book, it does not give much detail, i.e. it does not provide comprehensive step-by-step formulae to get things done. Instead, the entire book provides hints on what ought to be done and what ought not, leaving much of the details to the creativity of the readers. As we shall see later, Sun Tzu advocates flexibility rather than relying on any fixed method.

BASIC APPROACHES

In order that we get the best from this study of Sun Tzu's work, it is necessary to adopt the following five basic approaches – serious approach; contingency approach; multidisciplinary approach; human resource approach; and systems approach.

Serious Approach

This study should by no means be undertaken in a light-hearted vein such as for amusement, the way one reads Chinese legends or folk tales. Even the narrative given earlier (see *Introducing Sun Tzu And The Art Of War*) of how Sun Tzu overcame resistance in the training of Prince He Lu's concubines, has a modern-day parallel. An example is the all-common resistance of long-serving workers (who often are favorites of the founder-boss because they have been around together with him since the day the company first started) against a new manager brought in to introduce change on a scale which the company needs for progress.

As the opening sentences of Sun Tzu's work has warned:

The Art of War is of vital importance to the State; the way of life or death; the road to safety or ruin. It is essential that it is seriously studied.

Since managing a business is a serious matter, we should therefore look at our daily effort in managing as a sort of warfare and treat our work as a serious exercise instead of merely a "9-to-5" job. It is only with this frame of mind that we can study Sun Tzu's work with confidence and enthusiasm to maximize our learning.

Contingency Approach

Traditionally, management relied on certain established principles which provide a "one-best way" of managing. An example could be found in the writings of practitioners like Henri Fayol whose 14 universal principles of management prescribe the correct way to delegate, divide work, and to organize, etc. Going by the contingency approach, we shall accept that work situations tend to be far more complex and therefore we have to be flexible in applying practices to suit changing circumstances.

In emphasizing this need to be flexible, Sun Tzu uses water as the metaphor to illustrate this point:

As water shapes its flow accordingly to the ground, an army wins by relating to the enemy it faces. Just as water retains no constant shape, in war there shall be no constant condition. Thus, the one who can modify his tactics according to the enemy situation shall be victorious and may be called the divine commander.

By taking the contingency approach, I am therefore asking you to totally discard the idea of a "one best way" of doing things. As managers, we should decide issues on a case-by-case basis and not rely merely on applying a fixed formula to every case. No fixed, inflexible rule can ever substitute sound business judgement. Hence, just as a general must exercise his total discretion in deciding what is best, depending on the situation of the war, so must we, as managers exercise our total discretion in deciding what is best given the circumstances faced in our business. Hence, for each of the tools in use for formulating strategies, no one is the best but is dependent on the situational variables.

I still vividly recall an incident in 1985 when a busy Kuala Lumpur-based sales manager delegated the chore of receiving and entertaining an important customer from East Malaysia to one of his executives. The executive who had previously on several occasions accompanied his boss in entertaining such outstation customers, followed the prescribed steps of fetching the customer from the airport, checking him into the hotel, taking him out for dinner at a good Chinese restaurant, and finally offering the highlight of the evening – either have a "good time" at an exclusive joint providing massage and call-girl services or go to a nightclub. It was rather unfortunate for the sales executive that his boss had neglected to warn him that the particular customer has a reputation of never closing the day without first reading some passages from the Bible. As a result of the executive treating this customer the same way as he had seen others being treated (with good results), the company lost the contract of this very customer.

Multi-Disciplinary Approach

Sun Tzu's work may be an influential military treatise but it has found as much, if not more, application in business. As a practical study, the Art of War has applications in many disciplines or fields of study. The fields cover an extensive range like Accountancy, Behavioral Studies, Business Policy (also called Strategic Management or General Management), Economics, Finance, Personnel (or Human Resource) Management, Management Information Systems, Marketing, Operations and Production Management, as well as Psychology, which in most cases, have often been found to overlap.

Therefore, in this book, you will find that our study of Sun Tzu's *Art of War* shall relate to various subjects. Anything that can clarify and show the relevance of Sun Tzu's work as it applies to management being practised today, shall be utilized. Since Sun Tzu's *Art of War* abounds with useful hints on what has to be done but does not provide details on how to go about doing what he suggests, we shall nonetheless go by his "eye-openers" in relation to today's context and employ modern techniques to make his hints work. In short, there is a mixture of old and new in application.

Human Resource Approach

This takes a developmental view of the organization's human resource which means helping employees to become better and more responsible persons. Just as people are important to the economy and protection of the kingdom in Sun Tzu's time, today, people are positioned as the main or primary resource in any organization and every effort should be made to develop them towards higher levels of competence. According to Sun Tzu:

> *A skilled commander conserves energy from the situation instead of wasting his men. He selects his men according to their talents and uses them to exploit the situation.*

This clearly reflects the underlying principle of recruitment and selection which is used by most human resource managers today. Other observations by Sun Tzu include:

> *Therefore, treat your men kindly but keep strict control over them to ensure victory. If the commands used in training troops are consistent, sol-*

> *diers will be disciplined. If not, soldiers are inclined*
> *to be disobedient. If a general's commands are con-*
> *sistently credible and obeyed, he enjoys good*
> *relationship between him and his men.*

and

> *Give attention to the well-being of your men; do not*
> *unnecessarily exhaust them. Keep their spirit united;*
> *conserve their energy.*

The above observations not only show an approach which builds on equity and discipline to create a climate in which people are motivated to work together, but also the commitment to effective communication for training.

Systems Approach

When we talk of systems, it is normal to conceptualize several sub-systems making up a system, and in turn, several systems being themselves sub-systems of a larger system. In a business organization, there exists a multitude of variables within, with each of them seemingly isolated and independent, and yet capable of affecting all the other variables in a complex relationship. Similarly, the same business organization does not exist in isolation by itself but coexists and interrelates in an even more complex way with other organizations within an even larger system.

Hence, the finance department of a company is responsible for that firm's financial system just as the personnel department is responsible for the personnel system. Each is independent of the other and yet interdependent since they coexist and must interrelate with one another. The firm's financial system, in turn, is tied up with other financial systems, e.g. the commercial or merchant bankers, buyers and suppliers, Treasury, etc. In such an open system, complexities abound. Such complexities can best be described by one of Sun Tzu's passages which reads as follows:

> *In battle, there are only the direct and indirect methods of fighting but their combinations give an endless series of maneuvers. For both forces are interlocked and using each will lead to the other; it is like moving in a circle – you will never come to an end. Who can determine where one ends and the other begins?*

In taking this approach, our study will demand that before we take any action or decide on any strategy, we must look beyond the immediate situation in order to determine the effects on the larger system.

SUMMARY

Sun Tzu's principles in the *Art of War* can be applied to resolve various business problems. In order to understand these principles and to be able to apply them effectively, our study shall be guided by the following approaches – the serious approach which means not taking the *Art of War* lightly; the contingency approach which requires the flexible use of different principles and techniques for different environments if we wish to be effective instead of relying on a "one best way"; the multi-disciplinary approach which accepts an integration of many disciplines to enhance this study; the human resource approach which seeks to support employee development and growth for effectiveness; and the systems approach which recognizes the interaction of all parts of an organization as well as inter-organizational dependency in a complex relationship.

FORESIGHT

One basic principle of the *Art of War* is that "We do not assume the enemy will not come, but instead we must be prepared for his coming; not to presume he will not attack, but instead to make our own position unassailable"

CHAPTER 2

Strategic Significance of the *Art Of War*

IN THE PREVIOUS chapter, we have already seen from the opening statement of Sun Tzu's book, that the *Art of War* must be seriously studied. Since "strategic" is a Greek word relating to the art of generalship or being a general, the modern-day usage of the word has come to be taken as something of great or vital importance. Hence, strategic management is said to be concerned with matters of vital, pervasive, or continuing importance to the organization as a whole, and this clearly supports Sun Tzu's exhortation for the activity of managing to be viewed with seriousness.

While some modern-day writers have suggested that strategic management is mainly planning, albeit a high-level one with long-term significance, yet others have taken the view that it is rather a process of doing than of planning to do. I am however convinced that Sun Tzu holds equal value for both functions and that the strategic significance of his work focuses primarily on two major areas – planning (i.e. to do) and the relentless pursuit of knowledge (i.e. doing) for managing oneself and the internal environment and external environment. Once such knowledge is acquired, it shall be used to develop planning in the formulation and implementation of strategies for successful competition.

PLANNING

Apart from his almost nagging call to search for information to improve one's knowledge, Sun Tzu appears to think very highly of the planning function. It is indeed this need to plan that one has to seek information as input for effective planning. In Chapter 1 of his book, *Art of War*, he says:

> *More planning shall give more chances of victory while less planning, less chances of victory. So how about totally without planning? By this measure, I can clearly foresee victory or defeat.*

And again, in Chapter 12, he reminds:

> *The enlightened ruler plans well ahead, and good generals serve to execute the plans.*

Indeed, I have always found that it is the aspiration for growth that forces a company to come up with a sound and viable business plan which defines its corporate objectives and prescribes the steps for attaining them. In his insistence on planning, Sun Tzu advocates:

> *Therefore, appraise it [the art of war] in terms of the five fundamental factors and compare the seven elements later named – so you may assess its impor-*

tance. The first of these factors is the moral law; the second, heaven; the third, earth; the fourth, command; and the fifth, doctrine.

THE FIVE FUNDAMENTAL FACTORS

Let us see how the five fundamental factors are related to planning:

The Moral Law

By moral law, I mean that which causes the people to be in total accord with their ruler, so that they will follow him in life and unto death without fear for their lives and undaunted by any peril.

Generally, I see this as the philosophy and subsequent behavior of the leader. Douglas McGregor's Theory X and Theory Y are good examples. If we adopt the Theory X view of human nature, i.e. the average person dislikes work and will avoid it whenever possible, then our action is likely to take the form of coercion, control, direction, and threats of punishment in getting our subordinates to work. McGregor has however suggested that Theory Y – the average person not only does not dislike work but can exercise self-direction and self-control at work – is more appropriate to the pursuit of organization effectiveness. Therefore, I take the moral law to reflect the role of managers in managing their staff well so as to motivate them to excel in their commitment and productivity by first treating them with respect and fairness in order that they will reciprocate in turn. Treat your men with contempt or cheat them of their dues and you may soon find yourself deprived of their best effort.

In a more specific context, moral law can best be reflected in the organization's mission, i.e. the organization's continuing purpose with regard to certain categories of persons, such as the customers, employees, shareholders, suppliers, etc. Are we seen to be fair and objective in our dealings with these parties? Take for example, the way we treat our employees. Since arriving in Singapore in August 1991, I was impressed by the job advertisements placed by Seagate Technology International which not only declares "Quality people make quality drives", but also dares to publicly give credit to one of its employees who has won the 1991 National Productivity Award. Most employers would shy off making "heroes" out of their employees lest they become too "swollen-headed" or get snatched by the competitors. This is going beyond making declarations, for example, Hewlett Packard's "A leading company brings out the best in its people" and General Motor's "The employer who cares" by also ensuring the declarations made, are being acted upon.

Likewise, I believe the moral law also demands that we start out on any enterprise or project with the best or what we think is going to be the best, that is, commit early on to quality. This will reflect well on our mission to customers – only through giving customers quality products and services that we exist and prosper in the long run. Take as examples, Nippon Paint's declaration, "Quality paint that lasts longer", or Motorolla's "Motorolla Means Quality".

However, do not always take an organizational mission statement as the gospel truth. It is rather sad at times to find that management philosophy may not always be what we assume or believe it to be, but rather quite different from the company's declaration. This is usually due to the failing of the human factor in organizations. But it should not discourage us from identifying the continuing purpose of our enterprise. On the contrary, it is all the more reason that we should endeavor to fulfill such purpose.

Heaven

By heaven, I mean the working of natural forces; the effects of winter's cold and summer's heat and the conduct of military operations according to the seasons.

The climatic conditions imposed by Nature which generals at war must contend with, have been stretched into the imagination of the modern-day businessmen to the extent that terms like "business climate", "economic climate", "organizational climate", and "political climate" are commonly in use these days.

In terms of "business climate" and "economic climate", no realistic plan can ever be made without taking into account business cycles (e.g. growth, inflation, recession, or stagnation), investment trends which may be favorable or unfavorable, etc. Therefore, even though we may have developed a new product or geared to go on an all-out offensive against the competitor, we may yet have to postpone the launching because it may be a recessionary period where customers are not spending. Similarly, we must also contend with changes in the arena of politics, such as change of government, new legislation, or even *coup d' tats*, which may undermine planning. Hence, following the Chinese government's crackdown on pro-democracy demonstrators in June 1989, popularly referred to internationally as the Tiananmen incident, foreign investors were edgy for some time about the political climate of China.

And of course, the all too important human factor which is critical for the smooth implementation of any plan, demands that we work towards improving the climate in our organization so that our employees work in a warm, cohesive, and happy environment.

Earth

By earth, I mean whether the distances are great or small, whether the ground is easy or difficult to travel on, whether it is open ground or narrow passes, and the chances of life or death.

In my earlier book, *War At Work*, I interpreted "earth" as knowledge of the terrain, that is, where we stand in terms of the resources available to us, limitations and the environmental factors such as market structure seen in conjunction with demand and supply, pricing, the state of technology and the pace of technological breakthroughs, etc. Hence, in today's concept of globalization, "earth" is a prominent factor. When Nestle introduced a freeze-dried instant coffee to compete with Maxim in the United States, the Swiss headquartered management wanted to call the brand, "Nescafe Gold" so that the product could be marketed worldwide under one name, i.e. Nescafe. The "local" American management, however opted for the brand-name, "Taster's Choice" because they realized that Nescafe is not so well-known in the United States although in most parts of the world, it is the leading coffee brand. After two years of tussling over the name, the locals won. Today, Taster's Choice outsells Maxim ten-to-one.

In a more literal context, "earth" can relate directly to the choice of a company's location and such operating costs.

On the assumption that your location is the result of a historical "accident" (it just happens to be there), in planning for the expansion of your business or the extension of the current lease, ask yourself whether you are operating under a disadvantage in terms of transportation costs. Sun Tzu has acknowledged that transportation over long distances can have rather negative consequences when he writes:

> *When the treasury is impoverished, the causes being military operations are maintained from a distance; carriage of supplies for great distances renders the people destitute.*

Therefore, ask yourself how much you are now paying, for example, on freight shipping, and compare whether you could be paying less if your business were to relocate nearer to, say, the market and shipping destinations. If so, by how much.

Another determinant of location is labor – both its availability and cost. You can assess your firm's needs by looking at the product life cycle (see Figure 1) to determine whether or not you should capitalize on geographic cost variations. If your product is still in the development and introduction stage, you will certainly need all the engineering and technological resources available. Location should then focus on issues like the availability of skilled labour. Needless to say, costs in such locations are often high. If your product is already in the growth or even maturity stage, and thus ready for mass production, it may often be more cheaply manufactured in less technologically-centered locality where labor, rent and taxes are less expensive.

Figure 1
The Product Life Cycle

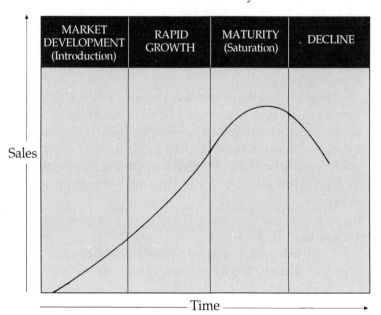

We must also consider the availability and costs of infrastructural utility services like telecommunications, water and power supplies, etc. Most of the investors who rushed into China when the communists "opened" their doors have been thoroughly disappointed by the country's poorly-developed infrastructural services. Take for example, Hainan Island which was one of China's poorest area. In 1988, it was turned into the country's biggest Special Economic Zone but for all the preferential treatment offered to investors, its backwardness kept most of the investors away. For the very same reason, while some people have extolled the market potential in "newly-opened" Vietnam, most are adopting a cautious stance for fear of hidden costs. Wages may be low but the skill level that usually accompanies low wages may also mean very low productivity. Besides, the inflation usually faced by a war-torn country seeking to rebuild its economy, lack of hard currency, and infrastructural facilities are other deterrents. In applying Sun Tzu's third fundamental factor, I personally take the view that Vietnam does not offer short-term profit though in the long run it may have interesting development. I also do not see it as a market because like China, people may abound but they may yet lack spending power.

Hence, if you must relocate, carefully analyze what the new location offers as a whole instead of just focusing on the isolated factors which have given problems at the existing location. And even if you cannot in the end get everything going in your favor, be objective in accepting that the chosen location could still yield the optimum advantage for operations.

Command

> By command, I mean the general's stand for virtues
> of wisdom, sincerity, benevolence, courage, and
> strictness.

Just as 'command' is seen to flow from a general, so must planning be perceived to originate from the chief executive officer. I have seen how some chief executives would totally delegate the planning function to their immediate deputies or some managers and thereafter keep aloof of the process and withholding authority. In such a situation, line employees could very well interpret a lack of credibility in the planning function ("after all, the boss himself is not concerned about the plan...") and tend to view the function as an intrusion instead of an important responsibility which should have been the way of life in the organization.

Wisdom

Wisdom means we recognize the need for top management's active involvement in the planning process. Wisdom also means we are able to recognize changing circumstances and provide for such in our plans. A lot of business problems arises because managers have not been sensitive enough to the marketplace to take precautionary measures accordingly. For example, the bitter lesson learned by American automakers who continued to churn out big petrol-guzzlers even after the Arab oil embargo had consumers switching to the smaller and more fuel-efficient Japanese cars.

Sincerity

In my view, sincerity means having an openness with our employees so that everyone knows their views matter and they should contribute the input necessary for effective planning. For example, a company which is marketing-based should avoid developing its marketing plan solely on input from employees in the marketing group but should also consider input from other non-marketing employees as well. Good plans can only develop if they are based on good input and a clear perception of what is going on where. Hence, we should listen more to employees rather than telling them what to do all the time. Chrysler's chairman, Lee Iacocca, is a man who regularly asks his people questions like "What are your objectives for the next 90 days?", "What are your plans, your priorities, and how do you intend to go about achieving them?" Do more than merely asking our employees questions such as "What's wrong with our products?", "What changes would you like to see?", "Where should our company be heading?" Take prompt action to screen and implement sound suggestions. Reward those who contribute good ideas and never criticize nor mock those whose suggestions are not so sound. The Toyota Motor Company is known for its 'Idea Olympics' at which the best ideas of employees are evaluated and given public recognition. In this way, employees can see our sincerity and be assured of the way rewards and punishment are given.

Benevolence

Benevolence will always ensure that we care for our employees, sympathize with them, and appreciate their effort and toil. This is an extension of the above virtue of sincerity. You will be surprised how the best plans can go awry just because the people who matters have lost the motivation to see them through. It is thus essential that a manager must keep faith with his staff. The moment he loses their confidence and respect, the plan is functionally dead. The lesson is the same as the one in the fore-mentioned moral law: treat your employees well and with respect if you want to get the best out of them.

Courage

A courageous manager will not hesitate to make decisions (even unpopular ones) which capitalize on opportunity. It also takes courage to delegate. I once knew an assistant general manager who insists he must have the final say on all issues – big or small – and yet lacks the courage to make decisions. As a result, all reports and proposals would pile up on his desk, sometimes for months. As more and more files would end up on his desk without exiting with his final approval, no project could get off the ground. When all the managers converged to chase for his decision, he would get all worked up and shout at them: "Can't you see from all these files on my table that I am very busy, unlike you lot who are so free?" As a result, opportunities came and went, creating a lot of frustration amongst the managers and soon one by one they started quitting the organization.

Strictness

If strict, our staff are disciplined because they realize we will not hesitate to punish. But to be strict with others, one must first be strict with oneself. This is what modern writers have called "leadership by example". Start by being a person of your word with small issues like keeping appointments, and honoring commitments and promises. In this way, plans can be made with the assurance that they will be acted upon without fail.

Doctrine

> By doctrine, I mean the way the army is organized in its proper sub-divisions, the gradation of ranks among the officers, the maintenance of supply routes, and the control of provisioning for the army.

Given that my basic training is in administrative management, I cannot help viewing "doctrine" as organization and methods. This is the way an army or a business enterprise is organized and structured. It is best reflected in the hierarchy as depicted in the use of authority and organization charts, operating procedures, policies, program, rules and regulations, and system of communication.

It is inevitable that any strategic planning will have to take into consideration the way the organization is organized and structured. For example, when Magnum Corporation Berhad – a Malaysian public-listed company whose primary business is the operation of a nationwide lottery game – decided to computerize its betting system, the corporate plan provides for the restructuring of its workforce from manual to technical, as well as causing the operating and security systems to be redesigned.

Another example of the necessity to modify structure in order to activate strategies is where an organization has decided on a product improvement strategy. This will usually require extensive research and development (R&D) and if no R&D department exist in the organization, one may have to be set up. When that is done, the R&D department head will have to know the reporting relationships involving his new department.

THE SEVEN ELEMENTS

And now let us look at the seven elements.

> *"Therefore, when laying your plans, compare the following elements, appraising them carefully:*
>
> - *which ruler possesses the moral law;*
> - *whose commander has the most ability;*
> - *which army obtains the advantages of heaven and the earth;*
> - *on which side are regulations and instructions better carried out;*
> - *which army is the stronger;*
> - *which has the better trained officers and men; and*
> - *in which army is there certainty for rewards and punishments being dispensed.*
>
> *I will be able to forecast which side will be victorious and which defeated."*

This checklist given by Sun Tzu for use in planning is without doubt, most comprehensive. When analyzed in conjunction with the fore-mentioned five fundamental factors, it covers the entire process of strategic planning:

Step 1:	determining the corporate mission;
Step 2:	analyzing the situation, i.e. oneself and the internal environment for strengths and weaknesses, and the external environment for opportunities and threats;
Step 3:	establishing specific objectives and policies;
Step 4:	developing the operational strategies which capitalize on strengths and minimize weaknesses in order to grasp opportunities and avoid threats;
Step 5:	implementing the strategies; and
Step 6:	monitoring results, i.e. evaluating the strategic plan as based on feedback for the purpose of taking corrective action.

Besides the five fundamental factors which provide guidelines on how to approach managing in general, and planning in particular, the questions which Sun Tzu asked in his seven elements provide very strong relevance to modern-day strategic planning. "Which ruler possesses the moral law" demands an organization to examine its corporate philosophy and mission. "Whose commander has the most ability", "Which army obtains the advantages of heaven and earth", "Which side are regulations and instructions better carried out", "Which army is the stronger", "Which has better trained personnel", and "Which army is rewards and punishments more certain", are all questions asked when one seeks to analyze one's position.

The answers will enable one to establish specific objectives and policies, and come up with the operational strategies which would allow one to capitalize upon one's strengths to take advantage of opportunitites and at the same time, highlight one's weaknesses in order to prevent threats from taking place. Once this is done, it is natural that the next step is to have the courage (one of a general's virtues as seen in the fourth fundamental factor, "command") to take the plunge – to implement such strategies. Another virtue, wisdom will see that the strategic plan is not taken for granted but the ensuing results will be closely monitored so as to evaluate the workability of the plan.

RELENTLESS PURSUIT OF KNOWLEDGE

Sun Tzu never lets up in his insistence on the need to pursue knowledge relentlessly. He is especially famous for the following exhortation:

> *If you know yourself and know your enemy, in a hundred battles you will never fear the result. When you know yourself but not your enemy, your chances of winning or losing are equal. If you know neither yourself nor your enemy, you are certain in every battle to be in danger.*

This quote by Sun Tzu has influenced Mao Tse-tung so to the extent that the latter has coined his own, *"Know yourself, know your enemy; one hundred battles, one hundred victories"*. The quest for knowledge is meant to be used in managing three broad areas – oneself; the internal environment; and the external environment.

Managing Oneself
A disciplined attempt to seek knowledge of our own strengths and weaknesses, what we can do and cannot do, etc., is essential if we wish to develop and manage ourselves sufficiently for success. It has been argued that if a person wants to manage others, he must first manage himself be-

cause once that is done, he will be ready to stop managing (since nobody wants to be managed) and start leading!

Managing The Internal Environment

Once we know ourselves well enough, we should start getting to know our internal environment in terms of the people, products, and other resources in our organization. First, get to know the players, e.g. superiors, peers, and subordinates, and how each of them relates directly and indirectly with us as well as one another. Next, find out as much as possible about all the aspects pertaining to the business – the products, operating systems, assets, liabilities, etc.

Managing The External Environment

No intelligent manager should ever view an organization as a closed system. Get to grips with the world outside – what are the current fads in society, which politician is on the rise and which one on the decline, what laws have the government just passed or are about to pass, what technological breakthrough has taken place, etc. Then, get to know your "enemy", i.e. the other person, or in this context, your business competitors. In short, take the time and make every effort to learn all you can about the companies and people you are dealing with, be they customers, competitors, financiers, government agencies, suppliers, etc.

It is only with knowledge that one can get the competitive edge over one's competitors. This has led Sun Tzu to observe:

> The enlightened ruler and the wise general can subdue the enemy whenever they move and they can achieve superhuman feats because they have foreknowledge. This foreknowledge cannot be obtained from spirits, gods, nor by reasoning over past events, nor by calculations. It can only be obtained from men who know the enemy's position.

In the beginning, this pursuit of knowledge is merely a matter of doing your homework. But once you have accumulated enough database, you should end up automatically using the information so gathered to "play the game", i.e. getting to know what people really want or convincing them to want, and thereafter attempting to give it to them, in return for some gain or other. But be careful – there is only one thing worse than not having enough information, and that is, having too much information.

As each of these broad areas is important, they will be dealt with separately in later chapters.

SUMMARY

Sun Tzu's work generally covers two major areas – planning and the relentless pursuit of knowledge. His five fundamental factors, i.e. the "moral law", "heaven", "earth", "command", and "doctrine", provide some guidance on what planners should do. Together with his seven elements, which can be used as a sort of checklist, they are found to relate to the entire process of strategic planning – determining the corporate mission, analyzing the situation, establishing specific objectives and policies, developing operational strategies, implementing the strategies, and monitoring results to evaluate the strategic plan.

His insistence on the need to seek knowledge encourages the gathering and effective usage of information to first manage oneself, and then, the internal environment comprising the people, products, and other resources in the organization, before moving on to the external environment depicting the relationship of an organization with its competitors within the social framework, the political facet, and the state of technology.

PART II

Managing Oneself

DISCIPLINE

This starts with self for as Sun
Tzu has advocated, "The good
commander seeks virtues and
goes about disciplining himself
according to the laws so as to
effect control over his success".
Hence, one must manage oneself
before seeking to manage others.
And to truly know oneself, one
must indeed be very disciplined.

CHAPTER 3

Know Yourself

BEFORE ANYONE CAN seriously think of mobilizing all available resources to take on his competitors and cut them down to shreds, he must first make sure that he knows himself well enough. Has he got the ability? What are his strengths? Or more important, what are his weaknesses which may jeopardize his effort? Sometimes a person may rightly believe that he has the necessary strength to launch an offensive against another, and accordingly proceeds to do so. But if he lacks knowledge of his weak defences as he continues with his attack, he may soon find himself in dire straits if a third party decides to join in the fray and attacks his weak points. It is thus most essential that we know thoroughly where our strengths are and where our weaknesses lie.

Sun Tzu is very loquacious on this subject. However, I could find no fault with him on the importance of knowing oneself, and knowing the 'enemy', i.e. those other persons that one is dealing with, if the ultimate object is to walk away the winner. It is such knowledge that will give one the competitive edge. In the business world as we will later discuss, everyone wears masks of various sorts, and they keep changing them. For example, people tend to act one way with their subordinates, another way with their peers, and yet a different way with their superiors. Even those within the same company tend to behave differently with those outside the company. The same goes for group behavior, e.g. social clubs, or the "old boy" network found in Britain. What then is the real self and what is the perceived self? One may get confused sometimes since one carries and changes masks so often in one's daily activity. Since business situations always come down to people situations, I find it essential to know the person I am dealing with. But such knowledge may be useless to me if I do not know myself well enough to be able to capitalize on it. When Sun Tzu talks about how one can make oneself invincible and yet only the enemy can make himself vulnerable, he ends up saying:

> *Therefore one may know how to win and yet is unable to do it.*

This quote never fails to bring to my mind a financially "street-smart" friend of mine who not only devises a complicated filing system but is equally industrious in collecting information on just anything that goes on in the stock market. For all the information he has got on his fingertips, he has not only failed to make any money on securities but has been "burned"a number of times. The problem with him is that he refuses to believe what many people (including yours truly) have been trying so hard to tell him: that he has fixed habits when it comes to buying or selling stocks – he rushes to sell but hesitates when buying. As such, he tends to pick up stocks when the price has risen quite considerably and yet always he is among the first to throw when the market starts moving. I hope he reads this and realizes he must overcome such faith to his fixed habits and be more flexible.

SELF-DISCIPLINE

To truly know oneself, one has to be very disciplined. Sun Tzu has this to say:

> *The good commander seeks virtues and goes about disciplining himself according to the laws so as to effect control over his success.*

Self-discipline is very important because people generally likes to live in self-delusion. Like my stock market friend: although he is far from rich in his speculations, he nonetheless believes he will strike the jackpot one day just because he knows a lot of what is going on in the stock market.

To discipline ourselves, we must first learn to be honest with ourselves. For example, in the use of personality self-tests which behavioral scientists like William Reddin, Robert Blake and Jane Moulton, etc., have developed, it is not surprising that quite a number of people have at one time or another conveniently indicated answers which are perceived to give a better rating of oneself instead of settling for answers which would result in minus-points. Similarly, honesty also demands that we develop an objectivity towards criticisms from others. This is because no man likes to be told any unpleasant truth about himself. And since we usually cannot see our own behavior, that leaves only those closest to us to tell us any of our bad habits or traits.

It is also ironical that although many people are quite perceptive in knowing what they should say, when to say or when not to say certain things, in the end they still cannot help blurting out some indiscretion or cannot control the urge to tell things as they are even though they are aware such would be detrimental to their interest.

In addition, there are countless gifted executives who simply lack the necessary initiative to put their ideas, convictions and dreams into practice. It is not good enough claiming we have ambitions if in the end we still fail to take any action to realize these ambitions. Much effort and sacrifice would be demanded because a manager can only develop success by first developing himself. Self-discipline is thus essential if we are to break from the easier albeit non-productive routines of hesitating to do something (claiming "heck, it's impossible!"), procrastinating something which ought to be done immediately ("there's always tomorrow"), or waiting for someone else to take the lead ("the timing is just not right"), etc. Start practising self-discipline right now by working on that tedious task (whatever it may be) which you have been procrastinating out of dread or simply laziness.

STRENGTHS TO CULTIVATE

Earlier in my interpretation of "command", (one of the five fundamental factors), we have seen how Sun Tzu extols the five desirable virtues which a general must have. Given its importance, allow me to repeat:

> *By command, I mean the general's stand for the virtues of wisdom, sincerity, benevolence, courage, and strictness.*

Again, going by the explanations which I have offered pertaining to the said qualities of wisdom, sincerity, benevolence, courage, and strictness, ask yourself whether you possess all these five attributes. If you are short of any of these desirable qualities, it is high time you start making an effort to acquire and develop them. As one of my school-teachers used to tell me: "What you don't know is not a sin; but when you realize that you don't know, and you still don't bother to find out to improve yourself, that is a sin!"

WEAKNESSES TO AVOID

Just as there are strengths to cultivate, there are also weaknesses which we should try to avoid. Having exhorted us on the necessity to possess the five virtues, Sun Tzu warns:

> *There are five dangerous faults which a general should not have in his character. Recklessness leads to destruction; cowardice ends in capture; quick temper enables you to make him look foolish; delicacy in honor causes sensitivity to shame; overly compassionate for his men exposes him to worry and harassment. These five faults in a general can seriously ruin military operations.*

Recklessness

While one should be quick and decisive in making decisions, one should not be reckless by acting merely on impulse and without planning. Good planning calls for the gathering of essential information for a thorough analysis so that we can weigh all the pros and cons before deciding on the action to take. There is thus a high probability that those who are reckless are often poor listeners. After all, since reckless types are those who would insist on getting things done fast without giving much thought to the issues or consequences, they would hardly bother to stop to listen to advice or opinions. Eventually, no one will offer any advice or opinion to themand this will be the start of the communication block.

Cowardice

On the other hand, one should not over-study an issue with the result that one ends up making a decision which is no longer opportune. By being too cautious, opportunities may then escape us. And since we hesitate to act even when the time is ripe, our secret plans may soon come to be exposed and by then competitors may get to know what we are up to. In the previous chapter, I have told you the story of the assistant general manager who dare not make decisions although he is most insistent that all matters must get his final approval. If he has more guts to delegate and trust his subordinates to get on with their jobs while he decides only those issues that matter, he could have spared himself the ignominy of being fired eventually when all projects came to a standstill and most of his executives had resigned in frustration.

Quick Temper

Sun Tzu cautions against temper on many occasions as evidenced in the following passages:

> If the general cannot control his anger and send his soldiers to swarm up the walls [of a besieged city], then one-third of the troops will be killed without taking the city.

and again,

> No ruler should put troops into the field because he is angry; no general should fight because he is resentful. Move when there is benefit to be gained, quit when there is no more advantage. For an angry man can later become happy, a resentful man become pleased, but a kingdom once destroyed can never be restored nor the dead be brought back to life.

Therefore, try to curb our temper for we tend to lose control when we are in a rage, thus placing ourselves in a highly vulnerable position for foolish scenes. Keeping a tight rein on our emotion will also prevent our feeling of agitation, disappointment, or impatience, suffered in one period from "spilling over" to the next. I once heard a story about a sales manager who got into a tantrum over some mistakes made by his secretary. As she left his room after a severe reprimand, his telephone rang. It was from one of the customers who called to place an order but later changed his mind and switched to another supplier because the sales manager was unable to prevent his irritation from creeping into the phone call.

Delicacy In Honor

It is also a mistake to be overly sensitive of our self-image. Some people called this phenomenon, 'ego' which is the reason why some things that should happen, do not; and some things that should not happen, do. I have a friend who is a brilliant financial analyst. When he was once interviewed for a job, he realized he was not going to get it because one of the directors interviewing him openly showed his hostility. After the interview, my friend thought it over and suspected the hostility could be due to his paying more attention to the second director and also for having failed to address the first director as 'Datuk' (an honorific Malaysian title). My friend subsequently joined another medium-sized company as a manager to end up within two years as its managing director. Today, through his efforts, the company has grown considerably. Just think of what the first company had lost because of the ego of one of its directors.

However, do not confuse a giant or "blown-up" ego with a strong one. Hence, a man who thinks too highly of himself is more often than not covering up for a low self-image. It is usually the ones who keep a low profile, can laugh at themselves and are not unduly worried about "losing face" that possess the really strong egos. These are usually the top executives whose willingness to take reasonable risks and objectivity to decision-making, would get things done without much waste of time. They have learned to be honest with themselves in accepting criticisms. As they are not concerned about "losing face", they are able to admit, "I don't know" without feeling inadequate when they are truly stumped for facts, or "I'm sorry" when they are wrong.

Overly Compassionate

And while we should care for our men, we should avoid trying to please everyone and end up pleasing no one. Be prepared to make unpopular decisions if such are necessary to resolve the problem. If there are several unpopular decisions, take them all at once because one bombshell is easier to accept than an ongoing series of unpopular remedies.

In 1988, when Magnum Corporation Berhad decided to go "on-line" with its nationwide betting system, the jobs of about 80 manual ticket-checkers were made redundant. The affected employees and their union representatives had guessed long before the board's decision that their jobs would be affected and had requested for an early warning. Against the natural instinct to procrastinate such negative issues, I called in the union representatives and key informal leaders to tell them what the board had decided and to discuss all other possibilities like transfer to other jobs or subsidiaries, retraining, etc. Even then, about 60 workers would still have to go, and we agreed to carry out the retrenchment exercise in two phases, with 39 in the first phase, and the rest in the second. We also worked out the compensation payments and the assurance of company's assistance in helping them look for jobs elsewhere. As a result of working closely with the employees and being open with them, the first lay-off exercise (which I handled before leaving to join another organization) went off without any bad feelings or industrial action. This example is given to show that despite the popular perception of Malaysian unionism to be "militant" and comprising a bunch of "trouble-makers", in reality, problems can be resolved amicably if people stick to principles of openness and sincerity instead of merely trying to "look good".

LEADERSHIP BY EXAMPLE

The cultivation and possession of the five virtues and avoidance of the five faults actually culminates in the concept of leadership by example. In another part of his book, Sun Tzu also says:

> *When the general is morally weak and lacks authority; when his instructions are not clear; when there are no consistent rules to guide both officers and men, and the ranks are slovenly formed, the result is disorganization.*

This is the reason why earlier in this chapter, I start off with the call to develop self-discipline. If we want to demand good performance from our employees, we must first demand the best from ourselves. Do not set them any tasks which we are unable or unwilling to do. Let us assume that you have told your staff to report for work early at not later than 8 a.m. while you continue to check in, say, around 10 a.m. Do you think they will be happy to obey your instruction?

And it is no good saying: "So what, I'm the boss". Remember, your employees may appear to obey and not talk back, but they will certainly talk behind your back. Chances are their thoughts will neither be pleasant nor respectful. This is the surest way that a person can lose credibility with his men.

Here, we must also take note of Sun Tzu's lesson on humility when he says:

> *What the ancients called a skilful fighter is one who not only wins but wins with ease. But the victories shall earn him no reputation for wisdom nor credit for valor. For victories are such, they are gained in circumstances that have not been revealed and he thus wins no reputation for wisdom; and as the enemy submits without bloodshed, he receives no credit for valor.*

What this means is that the truly wise or brave is also cunning enough to go about unnoticed so that no one may know what he has achieved and therefore be alert to what he is capable of doing. This brings to mind a story I once heard during my journalism days about how a gangland boss who deals in narcotics stays in power. He has most of the high-ranking police officers and other influential politicians on his pay-roll. One day, the police chief told him that he has come under great pressure from some political faction to crack down on drug trafficking activities. The gangster chief smiled and advised the police chief to plan an ambush at a point along a certain highway at noon two days after because a certain car going by that road will be carrying some US$1.3 million worth of cocaine. True enough the police ambush nabbed the car, drug, and driver, to warrant front-page headlines in the newspapers and satisfy the troublesome political faction. This further cemented relationships between the gang boss and the police chief. As for the driver of the ill-fated car, he willingly took the rap without "squealing" on his boss, the gangster chief. While he did not know that he was deliberately "set up" to placate more powerful quarters, he, like all the gang members, believes in the boss's paternal and generous ways to any of his minions caught in the course of duty. The driver is ready to face the music because his boss will look after his wife and children well. This also affects the other gangsters whose loyalty to the boss became reinforced. Can you therefore imagine the consequences if the boss's "double-deals" are made known to all concerned?

Of course, since this is one story I picked up when I was a nosey journalist, the sensationalism of a "Godfather" character, drug trafficking, "double" deals, ambush (possibly a car chase followed by gunfight), are necessary ingredients for a good story. On a more sober note, I really ought not write this book: all my secrets are out for reading, so what else have I got left?

A PRACTICAL APPROACH TO STRENGTHS AND WEAKNESSES

Although it would be perfect to have all five of the above said virtues and none of the five faults, in reality, this could be a most improbable achievement. This has been most explicitly recognized by Sun Tzu who observes:

> *Invincibility lies in one's own hands but the enemy's vulnerability is of his own making. Thus, those skilled in war can make themselves invincible but the enemy's vulnerability is provided only by the enemy himself.*

Let me ask you this simple question: "who is the enemy?" Assuming we are both rivals, then obviously you are my enemy as I am yours! Therefore, we both qualify to this title, 'enemy', depending as they say, on which side of the fence and from whose viewpoint. In this respect, going by what Sun Tzu has said, we can make ourselves invincible (by cultivating the five virtues and avoiding the five faults) and at the same time can also become vulnerable (by not being able to achieve the five virtues and unable to rid ourselves of the five faults). In short, we are human... not superman, and should possess both good and bad traits albeit the balancing would differ from person to person. It is natural then to desire more good traits than bad ones.

Hence, while we should still strive for perfection (or excellence, as some modern-day management "gurus" have called it), a practical approach to strengths and weaknesses in the meantime could go along the following suggestions which Sun Tzu has wisely provided:

> *Defends when one's strength is insufficient; attacks when abundant.*

and

> *One who has few must prepare for defence; one who has many shall make the enemy prepare for defence.*

These suggestions simply mean not taking on more than what we can handle. Find out what you are good at doing and also your limitations. Then work hard at *both* improving your forte and cutting down on your imperfections. It is only when you are very sure of your ability and yet aware of your shortcomings that you can move to better your position. I once heard how an ambitious albeit incompetent trading executive sought out his general manager to ask whether the general manager would object to his taking over the place of the trading manager who had just died of heart failure. The general manager replied: "I have no objection at all but don't you think it would be more appropriate that you ask his undertaker instead of me?"

Since the evaluation of one's strengths carries further implications for corporate survival and growth, they shall be discussed in detail in the later chapters.

SUMMARY

It is necessary to look within and get to truly know oneself before one can seriously think of taking on the competitors. To get to know oneself, one has to be very disciplined so as to avoid self-deception arising from one's unwillingness to face the truth, inability to control one's basic urges, and lack of motivation to put into action the words we utter.

Sun Tzu suggests five desirable qualities which we must cultivate – wisdom; sincerity; benevolence; courage; and strictness. At the same time, he warns of five faults we should avoid – recklessness which we take to be the failure to plan ahead; cowardice which is seen as fearing to delegate, make decision, or take responsibility; quick temper which risks making fools of ourselves; delicacy in honor whereby one becomes egoistic and fears losing "face"; and overly compassionate by trying to please everyone and ends up pleasing nobody. In cultivating the five desirable qualities and avoiding the five faults, we see how essential it is to lead by example.

It is also recognized for a fact that it may be quite impossible to attain all five desirable qualities and having none of the five faults. Even then, Sun Tzu suggests that we should still identify our strengths and weaknesses, realize their extent and limitations so that we can take on only what we can handle and at the same time strive to improve our strengths and overcome our weaknesses.

AUTHORITY

As Sun Tzu has observed, a
general must first receive his
commands from the Ruler before
he can assemble his troops and
blend them into a harmonious
entity. Authority is therefore
essential because disorganization
would result if he lacks it.

CHAPTER 4

Being The Boss

SOME BOOKS HAVE put a negative connotation to the word
"boss", suggesting that bossing is an autocratic activity and one
should be a leader and not a boss. I shall however continue to
go by this old-fashioned word because it is simple to use and
could quickly bring to mind the picture of anyone who heads
either a few workers or even, thousands of workers.

While bosses are generally thought to be highly capable
persons who possess a thorough knowledge of themselves for
how else could they have made it to their positions, there are
yet some exceptions. Some bosses could have inherited their
positions. A few are said to have got their plum jobs by "outliv-
ing" all other potential candidates. Quite a number have been
known to have acquired top jobs as a result of "connections"
and "strings-pulling". Take that assistant general manager

whom I have been using to illustrate incompetence at the senior level. He got the job on account of his friendship with the company's chairman. In some countries where corruption is rampant, there have also been stories of people "buying" their way into senior positions, especially in the public sector. Then there are those who "talked" their way into top jobs.

Unlike the said assistant general manager who could not hold his job for more than two months after his mentor, the chairman left the company, any person who inherits his position, "pull strings" to get his position, "buys" his position, or simply "wrangles" into position, could often enjoy his position for a considerable length of time. This could be due to several factors – the strong foundation of the company which despite being eroded by one's incompetences, is however solid enough to withstand anything less than a major crisis; the abuse of power by those in positions who could easily pass the blame to their subordinates, etc.

Although some of these "back door" bosses are quite capable and can contribute to their organizations, most however could only spell trouble for their organizations. While some organizations would collapse very fast, yet others whose foundation is stronger may still be able to suffer the mismanagement for years before they too would collapse.

THE RESPONSIBILITY OF A BOSS

Being a boss – over a team, section, department, division, company, or conglomerate – is therefore a very responsible position. This has led Sun Tzu to say:

> A general is like the spoke of a wheel. If the connection is tied and complete, the wheel will be strong and so will be the State; if the connection is defective, then the State will be weak.

I have already mentioned Chrysler's chairman Lee Iacocca earlier in Chapter 2. In his bestselling autobiography, *Iacocca*, he reveals that he regularly asks his people questions like: "What are your objectives for the next 90 days?" "What are your plans, your priorities, your hopes?" and "how do you intend to go about achieving them?" That way, he says, he keeps them in touch with their goals and dreams so that they become accountable to their bosses as well as themselves. Bosses like Iacocca tend to know what is going on in their organizations.

Thereafter, Sun Tzu warns of three ways whereby a ruler (i.e. a boss) can bring misfortune upon his army (i.e. the people working for the boss):

1. *By commanding an army to advance or retreat,*
   when ignorant on whether to advance or retreat.

Some of you may have experienced such bosses who knows not the subject and yet would insist on having their say. Let us take again the assistant general manager whom I told you earlier. Given his indecisive nature, he ought not insists that everything must have his personal approval. When files, reports, memos, began piling up on his desk, his managers told me that he acquired the bad habit of preferring to act only on petty issues, such as checking administration on why medical costs have run up, which company car to buy, and for whom, etc. In major issues, he was unable to make right decisions: by hesitating, he lost several opportunities to acquire potential businesses for the company, and ended up launching a couple of new projects only after the competitors had successfully launched theirs; and by acting too fast, he committed the company to a financing source which offers unattractive interest rates.

In another case, a managing director I know who was appointed by virtue of his having retired as a top-ranking government official, which made his knowledge of the particular government agency and his "influence" invaluable to the organization. He believes in running the business in the same bureaucratic way he used to run his department. The "red tapes" reached a critical point when customers could not get their orders on time because the salesmen failed to submit their documentation according to "standard procedures". It took the owners two years to find out the mess the company had got into.

> 2. *By trying to administer an army the same way he administers a kingdom, when ignorant of military affairs.*

There should be a proper distinction between line managers (those who have direct responsibility for decisions relating to the business) and staff managers (those providing specialist advice and services to assist line departments). I personally feel such a distinction will enable line managers to resort to expediency and flexibility unlike the staff managers' preference for set procedures.

I know a boss who started as a bookkeeper and because he was a relative of the owner, he was subsequently given the company to manage. As the business is mainly engaged in producing and selling a fast-moving consumer product, he has two managers to look after the sales function. Given his non-managerial background, the two managers' areas of responsibility were not clearly spelt out and instead they were left to sort matters out themselves. This resulted in some conflict between the two managers. To make matters worse, the boss favours the elderly manager who, like him, started from rank-and-file as a clerk, over the younger manager who has a tertiary education.

When the latter tries to change the firm's stand from a production-oriented one ("we make what we know best and try to sell it") to the marketing concept ("we find out what the customers need and satisfy this need for a profit"), his boss whose only concern is keeping the accounts books in order and not marketing, said: "Forget it! Our wholesalers have known me for so long, they will always buy from us. Come to think of it, why do you always go out to visit them? You should stay more often in the office to help prepare the invoices and phone them to chase after payments. I am always in the office and they come to me if they want to see me. After all, they need our products."

Shortly after, the young sales manager left. As the years passed and the competitors could meet the customers' needs better, the company's sales started to decline.

> 3. *By using the army officers without discrimina-*
> *tion, when ignorant of the military principle of*
> *being flexible with circumstances, This causes*
> *doubts in the minds of the officers.*

There are some bosses who seem to favour certain individuals to resolve their problems, irrespective of their assigned functions or what these individuals really know or can do.

In the case of a prominent executive director of a public-listed company, she always turn to her personnel and administration manager whenever any problem had to be resolved. For instance, there was a time when the company came under attack from the local press and consumer association for its defective products. The P&A manager was told to arrange a meeting with the reporters and give the company's side of the story. Needless to say, he came into conflict with the public relations executive who felt this should be her job, and the sales and marketing manager who also felt the presentation should be best delivered by her. On another occasion, the same P&A manager was assigned to accompany the finance manager to meet a prominent banker with whom the company was trying to secure a loan. It was quite natural for the finance manager to wonder why the P&A manager was tagging along. Not only did the managers feel confused and threatened but worse, the P&A manager soon began to act as if he was in charge of all the other departments as well.

WHAT MAKES AN IDEAL BOSS?

Sun Tzu has much to suggest on this subject. In his five fundamental factors, he has already touched on issues which are basically related to the human resource approach. A salient factor is the fourth, "command", where he extols the five virtues a general must have, i.e. wisdom, sincerity, benevolence, courage and strictness.

In addition, from time to time, he gives the following opinions of the ideal boss:

> One who does not thoroughly understand the calamity of war shall be unable to thoroughly comprehend the advantage of the war.

Such a boss will be prudent in realizing a "marketing war", if badly handled, can sometimes ruin a company and cause hardship on the employees. He will not emulate those who draw up marketing plans as if the competitors will not retaliate but will stand still to be hit. One with such awareness therefore tends to have the interest of his employees at heart and is capable of keeping things in balance. He will not, as the saying goes, rush where angels fear to tread.

> A general is like the spoke of a wheel. If the connection is tied and complete, the wheel will be strong and so will the State; if the connection is defective, then the State will be weak.

Even though I have mentioned this earlier, I am making this repetition because this is important. As the managing director of Nippon Machine Tools Pte Limited, Willie Lai told me: "When I know my men will give me their honest opinions of what's happening, I fear nothing." The trick then is to be "connected" with your people so that they give you their honest evaluation and not tell you things they thought you would like to hear. Being "connected" means being in touch with your employees. Such bosses not only knows the aspirations and feelings of their employees but also make sure they are in touch with the organizational goals, happenings and visions. Bosses of this sort know whatever is going on in their organizations and such knowledge means half the battle is already won. They only need the other half, i.e. knowledge of the external environment, and chances are they will get it mainly from, who else, but their staff who are ready to tell these bosses things since they are always ready to listen and not take it out on them even if they bring bad news. Besides, such bosses tend to go by an "open-door" policy and practise "hands-on" management. As employees of Bangkok's famous Oriental Hotel have this to say of their general manager, Kurt Wachtveitl, "...he is a leader who understands every section. He is a boss, a friend, a father, a teacher, and he knows which role to play at the right time."

Another way of keeping in connection is to reduce the number of layers of the hierarchy. The more management layers between the top and the bottom, the more the chief executive officer is isolated from what is going on down there, in the market, where it matters. The layers tend to filter out the bad news and pass along only the good ones so that when things start to go bad, the CEO is often the last one to know. This is why many large corporations are now opting for flatter organization structures.

> *Thus, the general who advances without coveting fame and withdraws without fearing disgrace, but whose sole intention is to protect the people and serve his ruler, is the precious jewel of the State.*

With such bosses, it is the company's interest that comes first. Whatever they do is for the best of their organization rather than in service of their own personal interest. However, in the corporate world, many senior executives unfortunately allow their personal agendas keep them from doing what they are paid high salaries to do – making bold moves to improve and/or strengthen their corporation's position. Their way of thinking often takes this line: "why take risks when we are already enjoying a high salary and comfortable lifestyle with only a couple more years to go." Junior executives, on the other hand, often opt for "safe" decisions so as to avoid "rocking the boat" and jeopardizing their progress up the corporate ladder. See how negative things can be when one starts thinking of what is good for oneself and only after that, for the company. One of the reasons behind the Japanese success story is their "management by consensus" system which effectively blocks the personal agenda factor. Japanese executives are reputed to think of their corporations first, and themselves, second. Hence, success of the corporation is attributed to the effort of every employee rather than focusing on an individual hero.

Needless to say, bosses who think in terms of "I" rather than "the company" can be quite petty. I know an occasion where a salesman offered $500 "under the table" commission for each van to be purchased by an administration manager who was then sourcing the first batch of 20 vans for the company's maintenance fleet. The administration manager told the salesman: "Since we were classmates before, I won't throw you out of my office. But get this straight: whatever 'cut' you've planned for me should go to the total discounts for my company." It was rather ironical and unfortunate however that the boss of this same administration manager is a man who, while quick in cutting the expenses of others ("We must not waste company money on maintenance and repairs of company cars, or entertaining at expensive restaurants"), spares no thought in lavishing himself at company's expense (e.g. fitting the company car assigned to him with the latest hi-fi set, car-phone, accessories, and dining at the best restaurants) because he must look the proper boss when meeting the company's clients.

> *The supreme skill in commanding troops is in the shapeless command.*

and again:

> *Thus, when I win a victory, I do not repeat the tactics but respond to circumstances in limitless ways.*

These two statements go to show that the ideal boss must be one who in accordance with the contingency approach, knows how to be flexible in meeting and managing change. At Philip Morris, it has been proven that flexibility can lead to profitability. When sales failed to take off for Marlboro after its launch as a woman's brand of cigarettes, Philip Morris changed the target market to the opposite sex by bringing in the "cowboy" image. The result: Marlboro is today's the No.1 brand in the world – smoked by both women and men.

And a good boss of course should not be wasteful:

> *The skilful general does not require a second levy of conscripts nor more than one provisioning.*

Too many repetitions of the things we do or the mistakes we make are wasteful. This will not help boost employees' confidence or morale either. A good boss is able to avoid repetition because:

> *He wins by making no mistake. Making no mistake means already having established the certainty of victory: conquering an enemy who is already defeated.*

This means doing it right the first time. And only good planning can ensure this. Of course, as the saying goes, to err is human, and sometimes the best of plans can still go wrong. When this happens, find out why, learn a lesson and do it right the next time. One should therefore cultivate the habit of reflection. Every night before I sleep, it is my habit to reflect over what I have done or not done that day and mentally make notes of things that require improvement. I find this helps very much in my career and personal life.

To sum it up, Sun Tzu has this to say of a general's duty:

> *It is the business of a general to be calm and mysterious; fair and composed. He must be capable of mystifying his officers and men so that they are ignorant of his true intentions.*

Supposing we are critically observing two bosses. The first is not only cool-headed but also gives you the feeling that he knows what is going on but does not really shows his hand. While he hears you out, he does not jump to conclusion, and in the end he shows he is yet capable of acting decisively and fairly. Now let us look at the second one. He is easily agitated and often speaks without giving much thought to what he is saying. In a crisis, he gets worked up very fast and starts berating everyone even though people are trying their best to resolve the problems. Which of the two bosses would you prefer to work for? And more important, if you are a boss, which description would suit you better?

Earlier, I have talked about the boss who is "connected" with his people so much so that a two-way communication flow exists whereby he not only knows their aspirations and feelings but they also know the company's goals, happenings and visions. There is however an extent to the information which an employee needs to know. Sun Tzu has insisted on information security on the "need to know" basis as follows:

> *He changes his arrangements and alters his plans*
> *so that no one knows what he is up to.*

and again,

> *Assign tasks to your soldiers without detailing your*
> *plan. Show them the advantages without revealing*
> *the dangers.*

Some people have criticized me for supporting such statements. I agree that such statements appear to be rather "sneaky" and somewhat immoral. But it is not for me to judge what is moral or what isn't. Instead I am merely approaching these observations of Sun Tzu as he would apply them in warfare and as a modern-day top executive would apply them in business. To some of my critics, I have conceded most humbly that there is nothing to stop them from being upright and totally open (without any secret) in dealing with their employees. In fact, I have even suggested that they make available to all their employees the company's financial statements, marketing plans and other confidential papers, and to my surprise, they kept quiet after that. More on information security will be discussed later in Chapter 9.

SUMMARY

Although bosses are generally believed to be highly capable persons with thorough knowledge of themselves, there are some exceptions. There are those who inherited their positions, a few who "outlived" other better-qualified candidates, some who "pulled strings" to get top jobs, others who "bought" their way into top positions, or those who "talked" their way into jobs. While some of these persons are quite capable, most however bring disasters to their organizations.

Since top positions hold much responsibility, attention has been drawn to Sun Tzu's warning of three situations where bosses could bring disaster to their organizations:

when bosses who despite being ignorant of the subject, are yet bent on interfering in decision-making; when bosses try to manage both line and staff functions in the same way; and when bosses use their staff indiscriminately. Similarly, consideration has also been given to Sun Tzu's suggestions of an ideal boss: one who cultivates the five virtues; avoids the five faults; understands the danger of war; does not care about personal fame or disgrace in carrying out his duties; can be flexible in his ways; and able to avoid making the same mistake. The ideal boss has further been summed up as one who is calm and mysterious, fair and composed, as well as capable of keeping his true intentions and secret plans to himself.

PART III

Managing The Internal Environment

FAMILY

It is in the Oriental nature to treat employees as members of a large family. For example, most Asian employers take on the role of head of a family and the employees are good children.

CHAPTER 5

The Organization

NOW THAT YOU know yourself, you are still far from ready as yet to go out and tackle your competitors. This is because you have yet to gain absolute control of the internal environment, i.e. your immediate operating environment. When Alexander the Great succeeded his father, Philip of Macedon, he did not begin by immediately marching out to fight the world. Instead, Alexander had to crush a revolt in Thebes and then work on consolidating the rest of Greece before he could take on Darius I of Persia. This brings to mind Sun Tzu's opening sentence in his chapter on 'Maneuvers':

> *"Without harmony in the State, no military expedition can be made; without harmony in the army, no battle formation can be directed."*

THE JAPANESE LESSON

Having seriously studied the Japanese economic "miracle", I certainly believe that between a powerful external enemy and internal dissension, the latter is more to be feared. One of the major reasons why Japan has been able to survive her post-war economic woes, the 1970s' oil crisis, the 1980s' rising yen, to continue today to outstrip the rest of the world in economic competitiveness, was her ability to achieve internal "harmony". She has been enjoying an astonishing average annual growth rate exceeding 10 per cent after overtaking the United States as the leading producer of automobiles, succeeding the West Germans as the economic miracle-workers of our era, and launching herself as the world's leading supplier of advanced computer systems. To maintain or even, improve this position, Japan now needs to expand this harmonization outwards, especially to her U.S. trade partners. Only with external harmony can she hope to get over her current recession.

In taking a macro-to-micro view, it is therefore essential for us to appraise the internal environment most carefully with the purpose of consolidating all resources in general and harmonizing the human resources in particular if we want to be in the position to tackle our competitors. We will see why later as we proceed in this and subsequent chapters.

WHAT ORGANIZATION MEANS

In Western views, an organization exists where two or more people unite to coordinate their activities in pursuit of common goals. The internal environment is thus basically about the people within, i.e. the employees, and how they are organized. Japanese industrialists have long acknowledged this relationship. Since the Meiji Restoration in 1868, when the traditional Japanese family system was extended to industrialization, the impact of industrialization has not only been considerably softened but the behavior of employers has further been influenced to a great extent. Japanese employers, in taking the role of "head of a family where their employees are good children," are expected to give their workers paternal attention. And even if these ideals are sometimes not realized (there have been cases of exploitation forcing workers to strike in demand of better conditions), they did help to counteract the impersonal nature of industrialization.

In Japan, the system therefore is more inclined to be human-orientated. As Japan's "Mr Strategy", Dr Kenichi Ohmae has observed in his book, *The Mind Of The Strategist*, to the Japanese businessmen, organization really means people. Although Japan has learned about labor and its relationship to production in Western economic theory, the Japanese still regard labor as a separate factor of production. The concept is reached over time after a process seeking to create an industrial relations system that avoided the class conflict and labor unrest that is associated with western industrialization. In viewing workers as a resource no different from other high cost items, Kazuo Koike argues in the Japanese Economic Studies (1978) that companies are seeking to make the best use of them.

THE FORMAL ORGANIZATION

Since the internal environment is basically about employees in organization and how they are organized, our study of managing the internal environment shall look at them in relation with the organizing process. We shall start with the formal organization theory on which most of the writings on management have been based. The so-called classical school of thought which emerged in the late 1800s have laid the foundation on how managers should organize. But they are really nothing new considering that Sun Tzu has written some 2,500 years ago that:

> *Management of many is the same as management of few. It is a matter of dividing up their numbers and functions. Maneuvering a large army is no different from maneuvering a small one; it is a matter of formations and signals.*

and also that,

> *Order or disorder depends on organization.*

Earlier in Chapter 2 when we were looking at the last of the five fundamental factors, 'doctrine,' we have also noted Sun Tzu's suggestion that:

> *...the army is organized in its proper sub-divisions, the gradations of ranks among the officers, the maintenance of supply routes, and the control of provisioning for the army.*

These words sum up the classical way of organizing which have become almost second nature to most managers' concept of the "ideal" organization: one man at the top with five (or whatever suitable number) below him, and each of whom has five more below him, and so on until we get a picture of perfect symmetry in a pyramid-shaped hierarchical structure.

And when this structuring is done simultaneously with the assignment of duties along the lines of specialization and expertise (or function), and bearing in mind the span of control (i.e. the number of persons one can effectively managed) as well as establishing rules, regulations, operating procedures, and monitoring against performance standards, the ultimate structure will provide the basis for employees to work together in organization. In this respect, effectiveness will come from:

- people and resources being allocated to tasks;
- responsibilities being clearly defined by the use of job descriptions, organization charts, and lines of authority;
- employees being clear as to what are expected of them; and
- managers being in the position (since authority and power typically increase with each higher level through right up to the top of the hierarchy) to make decisions and solve problems.

ORGANIZATION STRUCTURES

To see how structures can evolve in an organization as it grows, let us consider the following illustration:

Let us suppose the Warrior Electronics Company started out with 30 employees to produce a single component for the electronics industry. It was the brainchild of its managing director, an engineer by training, who exerts his personal control over the business. As a qualified engineer, he acts in a technical capacity and is involved in the development and production of the manufacturing process. He also handles the financial, marketing and sales functions. Given the nature and size of his business, he sees himself as an entrepreneur and operates within what is clearly seen as a relatively informal structure.

But over the years as the business became more and more profitable and growing to accommodate 100 employees and more products, he realizes he has little time for each of the functions he used to personally handle. If his time is given to dealing with the day-to-day problems, he is unable to take on the strategic role of thinking and planning for the company's future. Eventually he hires additional specialists to head each major functions and to report directly to him.

This is the functional structure since it strongly emphasizes line departments.

A few more years later, the business has grown into one which employs 500 employees and the range of products has also been expanded to meet new market opportunities. The line departments now require additional specialist assistance of staff services, such as human resource management to formulate centralized personnel policy, while the production department clamors for the support of research and development. In meeting this latest change, the managing director finds his span of control too large for him to handle and he solves this problem by creating an additional level of management in the appointment of a general manager to whom the heads of departments shall report. The structure is still of the function type.

The company continues to grow in an expanding market. The product range is now extended with each product line in order to meet each of the highly specialized market committed to technological innovation. Each market must therefore be closely monitored and this makes it difficult to maintain effective centralized control. Considerable delays in arriving at decisions have kept the company from capitalizing on new market potentials. The expanded production on the other hand has resulted in higher employment levels, causing communication lines to become more complex. The company then decides to try out a reorganization based on product structure whereby each main product area will be decentralized and be given more authority to decide and act on its own concentration of specialist resources around the design, development, production and sales functions.

Since it only takes additional delegation of authority and autonomy to turn a product structure into a divisional structure, the company soon finds itself adopting the latter. This results in the establishing of a profit center in each division – based on product specialization – with the manager being made accountable to top management for its bottom line, i.e. the acceptable return on capital. In line with the responsibility, the divisional manager has considerable autonomy in relations to the activities of his division.

It will not be long when the company may find itself attaining a size comprising 5,000 employees and enjoying considerable market shares with its products gaining worldwide recognition in their respective fields. With advances in technology requiring computerized support in designing and producing related items in a complete package for the customer, the business has to adopt more complex engineering techniques which demand more coordination between various engineering specialists from the design to the production stages. The divisional structure may therefore find itself increasingly unable to take the required levels of communication and coordination, both inter-departmental and inter-personal. The result could be costly errors such as misuse of high-priced resources since problems are not being identified early in face of miscommunication and lack of coordination.

To resolve these problems, the company may adopt what those "pioneer" industrialists in the American aerospace industry have effectively developed in the 1960s – reorganizing their resources around a series of projects, such as having essential employees drawn from each function and department to form "project teams" to effectively "pool" their efforts towards problem-solving and innovation in the project they are assigned to. While the functional hierarchy remains intact, authority will however pass to the project teams where participation and teamwork are required of the team members to achieve optimum technical and cost solutions. This is the matrix structure.

THE INFORMAL ORGANIZATION

In creating the formal organization by setting up departments or sections in pursuit of formal objectives, management gives people at work a social setting in which they interact in ways not prescribed by management. People who otherwise might not have met are thus brought together as colleagues and come to spend more time with one another than they would with their own families. In this way, informal groups often tend to develop spontaneously on the basis of friendships, shared interests and objectives or some other common activities. Whether over cups of coffee, over lunch, or over mugs of beer after office hours, informal relationships easily develop where people gather together to talk about the company's problems, personal problems, how these problems are being handled, who is being a "pain in the neck", and how to cope with him, etc.

Apart from the social need to belong to groups for social interaction, a major motivation for joining informal groups is to get access to the informal communication channel, known universally as the "grapevine". This is because people generally like to know what is going on around them, especially if it affects their jobs. And since formal organizations often have relatively poor internal communication systems, plus the fact that management sometimes deliberately withholds certain information from their employees, it is up to themselves to contribute to the social gossip which the grapevine carries in satisfying employees' needs for information and sense of psychological security.

The problem with office gossip is that it is almost never about the good things that others do. A man (studies have found men to be just as gossipy as women) whom I used to work with, delights in gossip, especially in gossip which will eventually lead to conflict and quarrels among others. He is always there to pick up malicious and scandalous stories about this or that person in the office, and thereafter repeats

the stories to others under the pretext of an "objective discussion of what is right or wrong". He thrives on indignation and if you took his bait in voicing your criticism or
resentment, then he is truly in business and you can be sure
your words will get back to the person who is the subject of
the discussion. This will either lead to an open confrontation
or you will have the uneasy feeling of having made a dor-
mant albeit potentially dangerous enemy in the office.

Another undesirable by-product of grapevine communication is that of facilitating unconstructive complaints. When a
member of an informal group brings news, say of an accident which has occurred at a certain work-station whereby a
worker suffered a cut on his hand, such news would often
trigger off an exchange of stories by other members about
management's poor safety measures and uncaring ways,
thus fuelling resentment against management. And the
longer the distance where the news travelled from group to
group, the more gruesome will the news become until a
rumor comes about that a worker has lost an arm as a result
of management's lack of safety precautions. Imagine how
dangerous such rumor can be for the organization.

Sun Tzu shows he is aware that the activities of the informal groups can pose negative consequences for the organization when he warns:

> When troops are seen whispering amongst themsel-
> ves in small groups, the general has lost the con-
> fidence of his men.

It is therefore crucial that anyone who occupies some
position of responsibility – whether as team-leader, section-
leader, department head, division head, or chief executive
officer – must be in touch with his people at all times. Hence,
using the earlier illustration of how a rumor about an
employee losing an arm in a work accident, if you are in
touch with your people, you will hear the rumor the moment it started. Waste no time then in announcing the truth

– "An accident occurred at Station No. 7 this morning when a worker suffered a minor cut on his hand and was promptly given first-aid treatment. Management requests that all supervisors check their station first-aid kit and all workers be more safety-conscious at work" – over the P.A. system to kill the rumor. Follow up with a memo to all work-stations. This is being in "connection" like the spoke of a wheel as mentioned in Chapter 4. In this respect, Sun Tzu advocates:

> ...the behavior of the soldiers are matters which must be seriously studied.

Modern-day behavioral scientists have also advised managers to identify key informal leaders in their organization with the aim of cultivating them in furtherance of organizational objectives rather than having them in opposition. This is what Sun Tzu must have meant when he says:

> Therefore, treat your men kindly but keep strict control on them to ensure victory.

COALITION

In studying an organization as depicted in the management pyramid, with each level reporting to a higher level, such formal structure rarely tells the full story. Most organizations experience a form of management by coalitions which cut across the formal lines of hierarchy. This is what Sun Tzu has termed as 'fighting in intersecting ground' where he advises:

> Ally· with neighboring States in intersecting ground.

Since intersecting ground is said to be that as enclosed by three States, it is natural for one who occupy such territory to seek an alliance with the neighbors. In this respect, a coalition is seen as an alliance of persons within an organization which is not prescribed by the formal organizational structure. It can take the form of an "old boys" network whose membership comprises those who wield power in the organization and whose coalition affords for mutual support. Such a coalition of functional executives may exert strong influence and shape strategy formulation and implementation especially if the chief executive is weak. In his book, *Machiavelli and Management*, Anthony Jay's analogy of strong barons who allied together to force their policies on a weak king in administering the country is a most effective way of illustrating the implication of coalition. Sometimes a coalition can occur when several incumbent executives ally themselves with an incoming but rising executive because they perceive him to be a "force to reckon" in the future.

Another instance of coalition is when a new chief executive takes over an organization by bringing in his own handpicked followers to replace strategically-placed incumbent managers. This is usually done with the purpose of keeping the "old guards" in check and providing the new chief executive with both information and support.

The coalition process is best described by the following of Sun Tzu's passages:

> *In making sure that an army can sustain the enemy's attack without suffering defeat, use direct and indirect maneuvers. Generally, in battle, use the direct method to engage the enemy's forces; indirect methods, however, are needed to secure victory.*

The formal aspects (i.e. direct maneuvers) are what you are appointed and paid to do, for example, designing and running a management development program. The informal aspects (i.e. indirect maneuvers) are what you have to do in order to be allowed to do your job well. Hence, a friend of mine who is a training manager, often have to talk, first informally and then formally, to all those persons concerned (including those who can support his proposals to the decision-maker) in his projects so as to "sell" his ideas to them and lobby for majority support to push through the proposals. He is in effect forming coalitions.

Sun Tzu however has this to say about making alliances:

> *If we cannot fathom the designs of our neighboring States, we cannot enter into alliances in advance.*

Having noted Sun Tzu's exhortation to know ourselves and our enemies in order to be successful in our enterprises, this is a variation of the term, "enemy" – getting to know those whom we are entering into alliance with. Do you understand now why despite having known yourself, you are still unable to take on your competitors unless you know your operating environment which may comprise those whom you work with, e.g. bosses, colleagues, staff, suppliers, etc?

SUMMARY

Having mustered knowledge of oneself, one must still know one's internal environment before one is ready to tackle one's competitors. The ability to achieve internal harmony, i.e. gaining absolute control over one's immediate operating environment where the people factor is most prominent, is said to be a major contributing factor to Japan's economic success.

This chapter thus looks at the internal organization which is synonymous with the internal environment by taking both the Western and Japanese views of organizations. From these views, it is found that basically organization is all about the people within it, i.e. the employees, and how they are organized via their creation of structures, operating systems and procedures, etc. The formal organization whose purpose and tasks are embodied in the organization structure clarifies the roles and relationships of each level of the hierarchy. The informal organization, on the other hand, emerges from the shared activities, aspirations, and sentiments of the group members as they interact with one another in the social setting created by the formal organization. Like the formal organization, the informal one also has its hierarchy, leaders, and objectives. It also exerts social control over its members and creates its own communication channel called the grapevine which can result in negative consequences for the formal organization, thus warranting management effort to monitor the activities of the informal organization members. Managers' tasks should therefore include identifying key informal leaders and cultivating them to further organizational objectives rather than being in opposition.

Coalitions which are alliances of persons within an organization, thus representing a form of management which cut across formal organizational lines are shown to affect organizational activities such as strategy determination in an organization whose chief executive is weak. In the same way, coalition may be a necessary strategy for the new incoming chief executive who fills key incumbent positions with his followers to ensure access to information and support. In forming coalitions, it is important to thoroughly know the persons whom we are allying with.

PEOPLE

The human resource approach
is not unknown in China during
Sun Tzu's time for he has said:
"Treat your men kindly but keep
strict control over them to ensure
victory". This approach calls for
one to be fair yet firm.

CHAPTER 6

"People" Management

WHAT SUN TZU calls an army is, in today's usage of the term, the people in an organization and they can be the few staff in your charge as section head, the few supervisors or officers overseeing their staff in the department headed by you, or the team of managers in charge of their respective departmental staff, all of whom coming under your overall control as chief executive. Managing these people, i.e. the human resource is often the most difficult of all resources available to any organization.

RESPONSIBILITY FOR "PEOPLE" MANAGEMENT

Some managers feel they can safely ignore the "people" problems because these can always be pushed to the officially-designated human resource manager (or personnel manager) in their organization. I once heard a sales manager arguing with his colleague in the personnel department: "Look, I don't care how you do it. Just make sure Tom is out of my team. I don't want to see his face around here anymore. As far as I'm concerned, he's fired and if he raises hell, well, you're the personnel guy, aren't you?" This is not only shirking one's responsibility but also shows a most unrealistic stand taken by some managers.

Although most organizations nowadays employ specialist managers to look after the "people" function, line managers are still nonetheless expected to manage those staff who report directly to them. For example, the production manager cannot shirk his responsibility over the production personnel just as the chief accountant cannot wash his hands off his accounting staff. After all, a manager is often described as someone who gets things done through other people, and thus he is not only dependent on them but is also responsible for them. Human resource management is therefore not just the specialist function for the human resource or personnel manager but is an integral feature of management, that is, the responsibility of all managers who have staff reporting directly to them.

WHO HOLDS THE POWER?

A fundamental approach towards the study of people in organization is to assess one's position in relation to one's subordinates, peers, and superiors. Such an assessment is best done by viewing one's role in each type of groups – formal (whose purpose and tasks relate directly to achieving stated organizational goals) and informal (whose basis rests on shared aspirations, activities and sentiments as individuals interact with one another in daily work activities) as one interacts with one another.

You will find that behind this interaction of individuals and groups in an organization usually lies power and influence as the efforts of all employees are directed towards organizational goals. Power is regarded as the capability to exercise influence over the behavior of others. The exercise of influence means changing the attitude or behavior of others. The stronger your influence, the more power you shall wield and the stronger your position becomes. Who holds the power, and to what extent, therefore are important questions in assessing one's relations with other people in an organization. Those seeking to become effective leaders, i.e. in the position to influence others in their organization, can only do so if they have one or more sources of power. Two researchers, French and Raven have provided a useful framework in classifying five sources of power. Taken in the light of Sun Tzu's observations, one marvels how human behavior remains essentially the same despite the span of some 2,500 years.

Legitimate Power
This is the power base traditionally associated with a person's formal position in the organization's hierarchy. As Sun Tzu observes:

> *In war, the general first receives his commands from the ruler. He then assembles his troops and blends them into a harmonious entity before pitching camp.*

Without having received his commands from the ruler, no general can assemble troops. Similarly, no executive can start managing without having received his appointment. As the position allows one access to power, it is no wonder that this source is also called position power. Hence, when a manager is appointed to take charge of, say the sales and marketing department, the department staff will obey his work instructions because they shall perceive this appoint-ment as a legal delegation of formal authority over them.

However, real power does not necessarily rest in letters of appointment, documents and memos spelling out the terms of reference and areas of jurisdiction. It lies more in what a person can achieve in practice which means he can still find himself inaccessible to the power his position car-ries. Thus, a new manager who has yet to earn the respect of his staff or for some reasons, have lost their respect, may find he is unable to influence them in changing their at-titudes or behaviors. This is why Sun Tzu cautions:

> Secure the loyalty of your troops first before punish-ing them or they will not be submissive.

It is crazy the way some managers start acting autocrati-cally with their staff the moment they take up their appoint-ments. Their famous words often take these forms: "You do as I say"; "I don't care...;" "You're the boss or I'm the boss?" etc.

Reward Power

As seen earlier, we cannot merely rely on our position alone. Exercising legitimate power by itself is still insufficient for control. We must actively seek to motivate the willingness of others in accepting our influence. As Sun Tzu says:

> Bestows rewards without regard to customary rules...

Our employees must believe we are in the position to reward them for their efforts. Thus, we must be seen to have access to the resources, i.e. in possession of a "bag of goodies", from which to reward them. Such rewards may be the authority to hand out favorable job assignments, promo-tions, pay increases, bonuses, etc. Since one must have ample resources to be able to hand out rewards, this power base is also referred to as resource power.

Coercive Power

This power base works on fear which means our employees must believe we are capable of punishing them. Such punishments may take the form of official reprimands, less desirable work assignments, holding out on pay increases, cutting bonuses, taking disciplinary actions such as demotion or even dismissal. However, do take note of Sun Tzu's caution on the use of punishment:

> *Too frequent punishment show him [the general] to be in dire distress as nothing else can keep them [his men] in check. If the officers at first treat their men harshly and later fear them, the limit of indiscipline is reached.*

Studies of convicts have found that some have become hardened by frequent sentencing in their early years for petty offences, and stiff penalties for more serious crimes in later years that they are no longer deterred from breaking the law. The same applies to the workplace where an employee, if punished too often, the punishment process tends to lose its effect and the behavior of the errant employee could deteriorate for the worse. And when the manager responsible for such an employee began to fear him, chaos would inevitably follow.

Expert Power

This power base is not the monopoly of the management but is also accessible to the rank-and-file members of an organization. When a person possesses special knowledge or skill which is acutely needed, he is said to wield expert power. However, expert power tends to be narrow in scope because knowledge or skill is limited only to specific task areas. I know a computer whiz-kid working in an organization which started to use a new complicated software. He was very much in demand in the initial stages when everyone clamored for his assistance and advice since he was then the only one in the organization familiar with the software. Department heads who used to chide him for his long-winded nature, suddenly became very meek and patient with him during those early months as they tried to learn as much as they can from him. For a few months, he found he wielded much power over these people but once the computerization finally sank in, he realized he no longer carry the same clout as before.

Sun Tzu however warns:

> *When the common soldiers are stronger than their officers, they will insubordinate. When the officers are too strong and the troops are weak, the result is collapse.*

To be effective in his job, a person must know more about his job than what his staff knows. Supposing you have just joined a firm as, say sales manager, and you found out that your assistant knows more about your company's products, customers, competitors, etc., than you do. This is bound to create some problems in your working relationship with him sooner or later. This has contributed to turnover of capable staff in some organizations. Another problem of having too highly knowledgeable or skilled employees is that of the organization being held to ransom by the said employees.

On the other hand, it is just as bad to have a manager who is so much more advanced and dynamic in ideas and actions than his staff who would always be lagging far behind him. Although the staff may be fairly good employees in terms of intelligence and diligence, having a super-intelligent and super-diligent boss can also create problems in their working relationship. For example, on the principle of relativity, the boss may unfairly appraise his staff as simply incompetent.

Referent Power

Sometimes a person may do something for you, not because you are his superior who order him to do so, or able to reward or punish him, but simply because he feels a strong attachment to or identifies with you. This source of power which is often based on personal admiration means employees find some admirable personal characteristics, charisma, or good reputation in their bosses. Sun Tzu has this to say:

> Such a general who protects his soldiers like infants will have them following him into the deepest valleys. A general who treats his soldiers like his own beloved sons will have their willingness to die with him.

This is the 'moral law' all over again. Treat your employees with respect and fairness and they will reciprocate in turn.

CONFLICT

In our study of organizations, the people factor features prominently. People are however the most difficult of all the resources of an organization to manage because they are often in conflict.

There are many sources of conflicts:

1. Corporate and individual goals' differences;
2. Cross-purposes of different departments or groups;
3. Conflict between formal and informal organization;
4. Conflict between manager and the managed;
5. Conflict between the individual and job;
6. Conflict between individuals.

As we have already seen in the previous chapter and shall see in the next, most of these sources of conflict are rooted not only in the informal organization but also in the inherent differences in the thinking of people. The essential points to remember here are that conflict:

- arises when one's thinking contradicts that of another;
- is inevitable;
- is therefore a reality of organization life.

In remembering these points, it is therefore useful for us to look at some aspects of the internal organization which may in some ways help to keep conflict in check. Organizations faced with the inevitability of conflict brought by competition over resources, priorities and objectives, further reinforced by individual and group rivalries, can only attempt to manage the situation by achieving some degree of integration and control. However, you should not carry too much hope of totally eliminating conflict. Some control, yes; total elimination, no way.

STAFF MOTIVATION AND DEVELOPMENT

For his times, Sun Tzu has shown he was rather advanced in his concept of motivation as gleaned from the following insights:

1. The "Moral Law" (the first fundamental factor mentioned in Chapter 2) provides the platform whereby men who believe in one's cause(s) are more inclined to work towards such cause(s).

2. "Heaven" (the second fundamental factor mentioned in Chapter 2) which requires the building of an organization climate of equity, trust and cohesive team spirit will inevitably set the environment in which employees are more likely to contribute to the corporate effort.

3. "Command" (the fourth fundamental factor mentioned in Chapter 2) will lead to confidence in the leadership since the leader is seen to be wise, sincere, benevolent, courageous, and disciplined.

4. Sun Tzu's emphasis on rewards:

    In battle, those who capture more than ten chariots from the enemy must be rewarded.

and,

    When plundering the countryside and capturing new lands, divide the profits among your men.

and also,

    ...with well-fed troops, await hungry ones.

From the above, ask yourselves whether your organization is competitive with others in policies of wages, promotion, benefits, etc. It is strange that despite being aware of the saying, "pay peanuts and you will get monkeys", many bosses still persist in "short-changing" their staff. I have advised a top executive of a public-listed company against taking advantage of fresh school-leavers and inexperienced graduates by paying them exorbitantly low wages, especially when the rate of unemployment is high. Needless to say, my advice was given in vain and when times improved or when these exploited employees have accumulated the necessary experience, they will quit to join the competitors who would be waiting to sign them up at competitive wages for their experience and the inside knowledge they could bring with them. These competitors have mockingly referred to the said company as a "training" school for the industry.

Sometimes, competitive wages and benefits can make a man tolerate an otherwise unacceptable situation. For example, employees who may find themselves in conflict over any of the given causes, may hold back from creating a conflicting issue or situation because they value the organization's reward system. In Japan, although only around 30 per cent of the workforce enjoys "lifetime" employment, it was for the sake of this career security that they do not "rock the boat" and get into conflict.

Sun Tzu however also warns against over-rewarding:

> *Too frequent rewards show the general to be losing control over his men as only rewards can keep them in even temper.*

There are many bosses who reward their staff every now and then not because they are generous. On the contrary, they are forced to do so for they have not only come to depend on these staff but have no other way of getting them to work. Staff who are given salary raises every now and then may cease to become motivated. As Abraham Maslow has observed, satisfied employees tend to be less motivated than those whose needs are waiting to be satisfied. Of course, in the case of those who always want more and more, there shall be no end to their expectation. The moment the bosses are unable to meet their expectation, these employees will cease to contribute and turn their attention elsewhere to other employers who can pay better. These employees are often poor security risk when it comes to your organization's secrets.

5.　Sun Tzu shows himself to be an advocator of staff development when he writes:

> *In war, the general first receives his commands from the ruler, he then assembles his troops and blends them into a harmonious entity before pitching camp.*

Once we are appointed to our positions, it is our responsibility as managers to develop our staff. Be prepared to give them some of your time with the purpose of teaching them whatever it is you find that has worked for you. It may be tough on you at first but eventually you will find your staff will become more competent in tackling problems without having to refer to you. This will certainly take a load off your shoulders. Bosses who complain they have incompetent staff are all too often themselves incompetent in that they do not know what is effective and how to teach this to their staff.

6.　He also touches on training and development by saying:

> *Nourish your soldiers and build up their internal strength so that they are free of hundreds of diseases, and this will ensure victory.*

I have a tendency to associate the word, "nourishment" with feeding an infant so as to cause his growth. In a similar application, our employees can only grow if they are "nourished" with training and development. In this respect, are you giving enough priority to training and development? As a brief distinction between the two, training is defined as "...any instructional or experiential means to develop a person's behavior pattern in the areas of knowledge, skill or attitude in order to achieve a desired standard or level of performance" while development is said to be "a conscious and systematic process to control the development of managerial resources in the organization for the achievement of organizational goals and strategies."

When I was reading for the MBA at the University of Stirling, growing unemployment and the poor performance of the British economy were hot topics for discussion. Several authorities have blamed the lack of enthusiasm for training and development on the part of British employers as one of the main causes. Training was generally not regarded as a key element in a company's corporate strategy for as a 1984 survey shows, on average, only 0.15 per cent of turnover was spent on training which is well below the 3 per cent of turnover which is purportedly spent on training by leading employers in Japan, West Germany and the United States. The British approach to training was said to be 'front loaded,' that is, provided only at the beginning of a career. In recent years, studies by Mangham and Silver still found the attitude and approach of British management to training and development to appear as ambivalent and the linkage between attitudes and practice less than clear. In 1987, Charles Handy cites another survey which indicated that 36 per cent of middle managers have received no management training since starting work and further suggests that "management training in Britain is too little, too late, for too few".

This reluctance in spending on training and development often arises because of bosses' lack of faith in the principle of deferred rewards. As George Odiorne puts it: "You can't measure what I produce, so therefore just keep paying and paying for training, and have faith that what I am fooling around with today will have a giant dividend at some undisclosed future time." Trainers in most cases are forced to limit the programmes offered only to those which are short-term in effect, thus sadly leaving out the necessary investments in human capital involved in certain long-range development plans. Besides, in countries where labor turnover is high, employers often refused to invest in training and development for fear of subsequently losing trained personnel to their competitors.

The importance of this issue has led me to elaborate more. My final question would be: "Are you afraid to spend on training and development for the reasons just mentioned?" If so, then something is amiss where your moral law and your 'virtues' (of a general) are concerned. If you have been a fair yet firm employer and your employees have confidence in your organization's mission, you should not hold back training and development for fear of the given reasons.

I was recently disgusted with the negative attitude towards staff training as displayed by a group managing director of a public-listed company in Singapore who interviewed me for the post of group human resource manager. In his words, "when you train your workers, you are making it easier for them to walk out on you". I believe he does not really understand what human resource management is all about. Two other companies in Singapore however revived my confidence by their commitment towards their employees' training. The first was Astley and Pearce Pte Limited, and the second was Nippon Machine Tools Pte Limited. Both companies are given to organizing training courses on a regular basis for their employees. Notwithstanding the high costs incurred, should their employees be required to attend sessions on their off-day, the management would credit an extra day annual leave for the participants.

7. According to Sun Tzu, we should not unnecessarily exhaust our men because overwork is not necessarily productive work:

> *Give attention to the well-being of your men;*
> *do not unnecessarily exhaust them. Keep their*
> *spirit united; conserve their energy.*

If your staff are overworked, chances are high that they will suffer from burn-out. Take the time when I was promoted as general manager of The Mall shopping complex in Kuala Lumpur. As Malaysia's largest shopping mall, the complex opens daily from 10 a.m. to 10 p.m. For some 15 months, I worked seven days a week averaging 12 hours a day! No, I was not a super-workaholic case. Nor was it a lack of delegation on my part. I had a team of managers reporting to me and each of them was given authority to make decisions in his or her own area of responsibility. The problem is that The Mall is my immediate boss's pride and she would often entertain in any of the complex's restaurants in the evenings and during the weekends. And being the complex's general manager, I would be taken to task should anything go wrong in the complex. Although my managers and their staff are competent in their respective areas, in the hustle-bustle of a shopping complex business, things may still go amiss. As I refused to encroach on my managers' time after office hours, it fell on my shoulders then to stay back late everyday and even turn up at the complex "just to walk around or have a cup of tea in the bistro" during weekends. This was gross stupidity on my part – I felt no sense of achievement 15 months later even though The Mall won for the first time, the coveted Malaysian Tourism Gold award for "best shopping complex" category and renegotiation of expiring tenancy agreements brought in a hefty increase in rental revenue. This was a sign of burn-out and it was fortunate for me that I had by then accepted the offer of a place to read for the MBA – an eight year dream.

So do not unnecessarily exhaust your men. It is indeed a sound policy to have a five-day work week and to give your staff more annual leave as well as encourage them to use up all their leave. Some bosses see it differently: if their staff refrain from taking their annual leave, these are good workers. What these bosses do not see (or refuse to see) is that overworked employees are never likely to be productive. Professor Charles Burden, acting chairman of the Department of Management at Georgia State University observes that to be a good producer, one needs to have perspective on what one does. In his words: "If you work all the time, you simply lose perspective." According to Professor Robert Dipboye of Rice University, managers are just as prone to the general observation of blue-collar workers whose productivity declines once they push past eight hours of work.

8. And of course, overtime is as unproductive for Sun Tzu observes:

> *In the morning, a soldier's spirit is keenness; during the day, it gradually diminishes, and in the evening, the soldier thinks only of returning to camp.*

If employees are encouraged to report early for work, given the training to do an efficient job, and made to realize the rewards of productivity, they are not likely to idle and waste their normal working hours to frantically work overtime to make up for lost work. There are also managers who allow their staff to submit lots of overtime claims whether such work is necessary or not. Such managers are either ignorant about what is going on or just simply being dishonest. Dishonesty comes in two forms. First, even though they knew their staff need not have to work overtime, they still allow them to do so because their line of thought goes like this: "why stop them from making some extra income?!" And second, these managers dare not put a stop to their staff making some extra income at the company's expense because they need their goodwill. These are irresponsible managers who do not deserve their positions of trust.

9.   He further suggests entrusting responsibility to subordinates:

> *Put your men in positions where there is no escape and even when facing death, they will not run. In preparing for death, what is there that cannot be achieved? Officers and men will both do their best. In a desperate situation, they lose their sense of fear; without a way out, they shall stand firm. When they are deep within enemy territory they are bound together and without an alternative, they will fight hard. Thus, without need of supervision, they will be alert, and without being asked, they will support their general; without being ordered, they will trust their general.*

The work of McGregor and Likert has given some attention to this need to entrust individuals with greater control over what they do, as based on the concept of participation. This has to some extent reduced conflict between the manager and the managed.

10. In fact, according to Sun Tzu, a little pressure is good for the staff who should be trained to take pressure:

> *His [the general's] business is to assemble his troops and throw them into critical position. He leads them deep into enemy territory to further his plans.*

While we should seek to develop our staff, we must draw a line between such development and being a wet-nurse. Remember, our business has to improve and expand otherwise it will decline and die. Some risks should therefore be taken. We should therefore develop staff so that they are constantly encouraged to seek improvements, to try something new, and to take risks. And should they seek you out with the problems you have assigned them and which they are unable to solve, neither throw them out of your office nor start solving the problems for them. Be a facilitator by asking them pertinent questions which will help them see their problems in a clearer light. Then, let them make their own decisions. You shall, of course, be the final judge.

11. Needless to say, in all the instances as mentioned, authority must commensurate with responsibility:

> *If the situation offers victory but the ruler forbids fighting, the general may still fight. If the situation is such that he cannot win, the general must stay his hand even if the ruler orders him to fight.*

This will prevent people from becoming "yes-men" to their bosses. I understand not many bosses welcome opinions which differ from their own, and I know most people would simply say yes just to please their bosses. But if we are employed as managers, it is our professional duty to be honest and give our opinions even though such may contradict those of our bosses. We must always put the self-agenda aside and seek to do what is best for our organization as a whole. Recall the story of Sun Tzu executing the two favorite concubines of Prince He Lu despite the royal protest. If he had not done so, he would not have been able to train those concubines as he had done.

DISCIPLINE

On the topic of discipline, Sun Tzu is very clear:

Treat your men kindly but keep strict control over them to ensure victory.

If there is no discipline, how can there be control, i.e. the process of ensuring strategies are being implemented and going according to plan? This perhaps explain why some organizations in countries like Singapore prefer to employ those who had undergone military training under the national service scheme. In Japan, it is quite common for companies to send their executives to annual camps where they are given training under military-style discipline with spiritual and social overtones so as to enable them to learn to be humble and tolerant as well as take hardship.

But just as he warns against over-rewarding, he also warns of going overboard with punishment:

Too frequent punishment shows him [the general] to be in dire distress as nothing else can keep them

*[the soldiers] in check. If the officers at first treat the
men harshly and later fear them, the limit of indis-
cipline is reached.*

If an employee is punished too often or very often
threatened with punishment, soon punishment will lose its
effect and the employee may behave even worse. That is
why sometimes a domestic inquiry may find the same
employee "on trial" shortly after other previous hearings for
the same or other offence.

And watch out against practising favoritism:

*If a general is too indulgent; if he loves his men too
much to enforce his commands, and cannot assert
control when troops are in disorder, then soldiers
are similar to spoilt children and are useless.*

and also,

*Secure the loyalty of your troops before punishing
them or they will not be submissive. When they are
loyal and if punishment is still not enforced, you
still cannot use them.*

Some managers have double standards. One for disciplining those who do not come in their good books and the
other for those who do. If we practise favoritism in this manner, our staff will cease to believe in our capability to be firm
yet fair. This will not only spoil the favoured ones but will
demoralize the others. As a result, the trust that is essential
in a management-workers' relationship will be destroyed.

To be firm yet fair means having clear-cut policies for
consistency:

*If the general's commands are consistently credible
and obeyed, he enjoys good relations between him
and his men.*

By giving consistent instructions, we can avoid confus-
ing our staff, creating doubts and thus pushing them into

disobedience. A general manager I used to know caused his company to go deep into the red because he makes decisions whimsically according to his moods. This caused so much confusion and frustration that not only did things go wrong most of the times but the company was unable to attract or retain capable staff.

So watch out for the following scenario:

> *When troops are seen whispering amongst themsel-*
> *ves in small groups, the general has lost the con-*
> *fidence of his men.*

Such a situation shows discontent is breeding. This can easily deteriorate into conflict. This is a reminder of how we have to identify working groups and their key leaders in the informal organization which I have earlier described in Chapter 5.

SUMMARY

This chapter looks at the management of the "people" element in organization. It starts off by placing the responsibility squarely on all managers and not just on the human resource (or personnel) manager. Since power features in any study of people in organization, we look next at the five sources of power as French and Raven have identified: legitimate power, reward power, coercive power, expert power, and referent power. As people are often in conflict, we also look at the sources of conflict. Our study finds that conflict arises when one's thinking contradicts that of another, thus making it an inevitable phenomena and therefore a reality of organization life.

Sun Tzu's views on staff motivation and development are seen to be rather advanced for his times. The 'moral law' allows men to work for causes they believe in while 'heaven' establishes the organization climate. 'Command' which requires leaders to have the five 'virtues' will enhance confidence in the leadership. Sun Tzu has also emphasized on material rewards though he warns against over-rewarding men lest they cease to be motivated or come to expect more and more. In the area of staff development, his writing further reminds us of our responsibility as managers to develop our staff. It was thus emphasized that training and development are essential spending and employees should not be deprived just because employers may not get immediate gains and trained employees may subsequently quit to join rival firms. If one has been a firm yet fair employer, training and development will not only fulfill the corporate mission but will ensure employees' confidence.

As for Sun Tzu's suggestion that we should not unnecessarily exhaust our men, this shows overwork may not lead to productivity since men may suffer from burn-out as a consequence. It may therefore be sound policy to have a five-day work week and to give employees more annual leave which they should use up. Overtime work should also be discouraged as it is not only costly but may not be productive. Sun Tzu also suggests entrusting responsibility to subordinates and training them to take pressure. Such responsibility should also be given the necessary authority to go with it.

On discipline, Sun Tzu's views are such that it is a necessity if we are to ensure victory. He however warns of over-punishing because such will cause its effect to be lost on the person who is punished too often. He also cautions against practising favoritism since this behavior will not only spoil those being favored but will further demoralize the others. This calls for policies to be consistent and clear. Finally, he shares with us a sure sign of leaders who have lost the confidence of their men: "when the men are seen whispering amongst themselves in small groups". This is quite similar to modern-day informal group behavior which remind us of the need to identify informal groups and their key leaders so as to monitor their activities.

DOCTRINE

This character also in its basic
form, denotes "law", giving rise
to the way things are done or
instructions are carried out. Each
organization has its way of doing
things and as such calls for an
internal analysis if one seeks to
understand the corporation.

CHAPTER 7

Using The Internal Analysis Approach

NOW THAT WE have looked at the people in organization and how they are organized, we should next look at one effective tool which we can use to study them in their functional areas in relations to business policy and strategy. This tool, known as the Internal Analysis or Functional Audit Approach, is useful because it equips one with the framework necessary to understand the analytical process so as to be able to analyze an organization in breadth and depth. The objective is to identify and/or develop key strategic or success factors.

In short, it is about assessing where the organization has been (or what the organization has been doing) and where it is now (or what it is doing) in order to determine where it should be (or what it should be doing). This means looking not just at the people factor but also the non-people factor, i.e. other organizational resources. As Sun Tzu has acknowledged, while people (good generals and brave soldiers) are important to the war effort, yet more are needed for total victory:

An army cannot survive without its equipment, food and stores.

And just as Sun Tzu's Seven Elements have asked pertinent questions about one's army compared with another's, Internal Analysis poses several key questions which should be asked of each functional area. Some examples are herewith provided of each of the main functional areas.

HUMAN RESOURCE MANAGEMENT

- What is the attitude of top management towards the human side of enterprise? Has enough attention been given to portray its fundamental role in the managerial philosophies of the organization?
- Are the policies covering people associated with the organization clear and equitable? Do they give the organization the competitive edge over other employers in terms of wages, promotion, training, benefits, etc?
- How are these policies communicated to the employees? Do they see the management as being caring for their well-being which lead to a sense of belonging and corporate effort on their part or do they perceive management with suspicion of being paternalistic?
- What is the organization climate like? Does it reflect harmony, openness and productivity, or conflict, apathy and counter-productivity? What is the overall relationship between individuals and the organization?
- Is there a morale problem at any or all levels of the organization? Does this lead to conflict, counter-produc-

tivity such as absenteeism, accidents, industrial action, or high labor turnover?

- Does the informal organization support or counter the efforts of the formal organization? Is the management sensitive to the entire spectrum of human behavior and has it shown wisdom in dealing with these aspects of organization life?

OPERATIONS AND PRODUCTION MANAGEMENT

- Are the management of these areas in line with overall organizational objective and strategy?
- How does operating and production costs given in the financial statements compare with sales, both as absolutes and percentages? What is the key cost element, such as labor or materials? Has attention been given to their control? If rising, is this due to cost increases or cost-squeeze? Has any cost-control programmes providing up-to-date standards been used?
- Are there adequate quality control procedures? How is this reflected in the firm's reputation as regards the industry's standard and environmental conditions?
- What inventory levels (including composition of the inventory such as work-in-progress and finished goods) are you keeping? Is inventory rising beyond expectations? If so, why?
- How effective have the firm's production control and scheduling, as well as their communication lines been?
- Do production personnel get timely, relevant and accurate information which are vital to the production process from quality control, cost control, sales, and other groups?
- In the area of logistics, how are purchasing and materials handling organized and run in terms of their relationship and communication with produc-

tion? What is the situation regarding cost and effectiveness in this area?

- Are operation and production effectively utilizing management science, in general, and computer technology, in particular?
- Are plant facilities and resources adequate and in good condition as compared with competition? Is the equipment designed for single-purpose or multi-purpose and flexible usage? Is the plant highly automated or labor intensive? What are the latest development in technology? How will this affect future plans?

RESEARCH AND DEVELOPMENT

- Is R&D accorded a strategic role in the organization? If so, has the organization's commitment to R&D been effective? Is R&D a major and essential spending in the industry?
- Is the nature of the product emphasizing on continual development or continual advancement in products as consumer or competition demands?
- Is the organization concentrating its R&D effort on selected products only, or is such effort enjoyed by all products? To what extent can the organization afford to devote to the R&D effort? In case a breakthrough is achieved, what would the payoff be like? How realistic would the opportunity be in terms of risk and return?
- Is the R&D effort adequately manned by qualified experts? If so, in which particular area would the R&D strength be inclined, considering the concentration of expertise? Are creativity and innovation adequately encouraged?
- Are resources set for the R&D effort adequate and effectively utilized? Has R&D communicating and

coordinating effectively with marketing and production? Does the organization enjoy a steady stream of new products or improvements?

MARKETING

- Does the marketing function reflect the organizational objective and strategy?
- What are product market shares like and how would each of the products relate to the product life cycle stages as well as the BCG (Boston Consulting Group) Matrix of "cash cows, stars, question marks and dogs"?
- What are the organization's key elements of competitive strategy: low price, high quality, prompt delivery, service, long-term warranty, etc?
- What are the organization's distribution channels and how do they operate? Are they effective or are there new development in consumer demand or distribution to warrant consideration of whether to change or shift emphasis?
- Has adequate studies been made of sales volume and price relationships? Is the firm going on exclusive selling on low volume with high price margin or mass marketing for large volume with low price margin? Is the pricing policy intended to skim the cream or penetrate the market for more of the market share?
- Is market research being utilized? If so, does it affect the determination of what products should be offered and to whom, or what products are to be dropped?
- Is marketing policy in line with competition, consumer taste and need, technological change, and other social and environmental issues? How does marketing communicate and relate such issues with production and R&D?

ACCOUNTING AND FINANCE

- Does the accounting and finance functions comply with the organization's financial plan? Are the financial plans of sub-units consistent with those of the overall organization?

- Going by appropriate ratios, percentage analysis, etc., how does the organization stand in the analysis of its financial performance and status? Are the results favorably comparable against the organizational expectations or the industry standards? If not, are there provisions for corrective action where required?

- How effective are communication and coordination maintained with operations and production personnel, especially in the area of inventory control, as well as with sales and marketing, in chasing late credit payments?

- What types of reports are prepared and which managers have access? Are these reports timely, relevant and accurate? Have they been well utilized by the managers in planning and controlling their activities?

- Are computers used to support the accounting and finance functions? If so, does it provide useful and timely information or does it produce tons of paper print-outs that are of no particular value to management?

- What priority has top management accord the planning and controlling of corporate exercises such as preparation of the annual budget? Are people in the organization contributing or do they just ignore and/or procrastinate the effort?

CHAPTER 8

Office Politicking

OUR STUDY OF the management of the internal environment
will be incomplete without taking a look at office politics and its
management.

Many organizations, seeking to look good professionally,
have "buried their heads in the sand" in pretending that there is
no such phenomenon as politicking. In the cool, rational world
of executive decision-making amidst mind-boggling technological advancement, the subject is not only taboo but is usually dis-
missed as a nasty abnormality which competent executives must
discreetly eliminate totally from their organizations. Discreet is
the word since politics officially does not exist.

But this only shows how men enjoy deceiving themselves.
Since the interests of individuals or groups do diverge from
time to time, some kind of politicking almost always results. It

is therefore more constructive and realistic to recognize its exist-ence (politics will exist so long as man is not extinct), under-stand its nature to realize that politicking is not necessarily bad but could be good, and in this way, seek to keep politicking within manageable bounds.

TERRITORIALITY

Long ago, zoologists have found evidence of territorial in-stinct in animals. An example, is the male hippopotamus which marks out its territory by defecating all round its perimeter. Should any other hippopotamus enter that ter-ritory so marked, it will mean a fight to the death.

Basically, man is no different and tends to possess the same territorial instinct although his action may be less crude – we may not actually defecate to mark our territory but we nonetheless have a natural tendency to indicate our possession. I have observed with some amusement on many occasions how people (including myself) in moving into a new office would use personal items, like calendars, framed photographs, pictures, or college plaques to decorate their walls, and books or magazines to decorate their shelves, etc. Such actions are tantamount to marking our territories, i.e., "this is my office".

Territorial instinct also can surface when we are in close proximity with others. Some people are more territorially conscious in that the nearer (in terms of physical distance) you get to them, the more keen they feel your presence and often resent such proximity. This again depends on how welcome you are to them, i.e. whether they see you as a friend or as a threat. I quite agree with those "body-lan-guage" experts who warn that when a man crosses his arms as you inched towards him, that is a sign that he is "on guard" for you have either gone too near and is infringing on his territory or he is reacting defensively to what you are saying.

TERRITORIAL "POWER PLAYS"

Territoriality is thus the root of politicking since it arises as a desire to protect our interests. Whether as section heads, department heads, or division heads, we are bound to get involved more or less in territorial "power plays" when those working with us started behaving in territorial ways. Sometimes we may be the ones who initiated such "power plays" with others.

But if we care to be honest with ourselves, such behavior can be most unpleasant. For example, we would certainly not like it if we go to work one day and find that someone has moved the items on our desks, rearranged our trays, files, stationery, etc, or even moved our furniture about.

Similarly, how would you like it if a manager from another department walks into yours and without getting your consent, orders one of your staff to go to his car and carry a bulky computer terminal for the chairman's office? You would certainly be in a quandary – a part of you would be agitating, "Joe is my staff! You have no right to order him about!" while another part of you would rationalize, "It's all right, after all it's for the chairman".

A particular "power play" which has been etched into my memory concerns two directors. The first director announced an important meeting in his office-suite at 2 p.m. to decide on whether to go ahead with a vital project which had fallen far behind schedule.

The second director replied: "Sorry, I cannot make it as I have other urgent appointments already lined up. I could however find some time, say at 3.30 p.m. if you could arrange for everyone to meet at my office."

At about 3 p.m. the intercom lines got busy again as frantic secretaries tried to reschedule the meeting to 5 p.m. at the first director's office because an "emergency" had come up for the first director who was so "tied up that he won't be able to leave his desk".

While this particular "power play" came about because each director was trying to exert his dominance in the organization, territorial issues are involved: each director wanted the meeting to take place in his own office, i.e. his territory. They could have been secretly following Sun Tzu who has suggested:

> *Therefore, the skilful commander imposes his will*
> *on the enemy by making the enemy come to him in-*
> *stead of being brought to the enemy.*

This has been the universal belief that when people come to your place – be it your desk, partitioned area, office room, or corner of the building, etc., – for meetings or negotiations of any sort, you are in the stronger position. This is because you are in "home" territory where you are not only familiar with the layout but also have on hand, fast access to facilities of communication, materials such as files, documents, etc., and the service of your trusted secretary.

Territorial confrontation need not necessarily be confined to physical issue such as over departmental floor space, your part of the building, or even physical proximity. They could also erupt over other issues such as where another manager resents your "intrusion" into what he believes to be an essential part of his job. Thus, the computer systems manager may feel that only his systems analyst and himself are sufficient in interviewing potential candidates for the programmers' vacancies in his department. As the human resource manager lacks the necessary technical knowledge, his presence and involvement in the selection process is thus viewed as an intrusion and a nuisance.

HANDLING TERRITORIAL CONFRONTATION

The first thing you have to do is recognize the seriousness of territorial confrontations. Even though territorial confrontations may appear to be silly and the actions of those behaving in territorial ways may even seem funny, when viewed by those who are not involved directly and whose territories are not threatened, they are no laughing matter. I have known a few managers who have taken their subordinates' territorial confrontations lightly, to wish later that they have been more serious instead. In one incident, two car salesmen not only ended up in a physical fight in the office causing considerable damage to the company's properties but also succeeded in chasing away a number of customers who were put off by the conduct of these two "warring" salesmen.

Territorial confrontation is a serious matter because to the aggrieved party – i.e. the one whose territory is threatened – it is no laughing matter. The urge to repel the "invader" or "invaders" by any mean is great because if one starts to back down, he can be seen by other employees as weak and submissive.

Remember earlier in Chapter 4 when we were discussing the ideal boss, I quoted Sun Tzu as saying:

> One who does not thoroughly understand the calamity of war shall be unable to thoroughly comprehend the advantage of the war.

This principle aptly applies here. Once you have recognized the seriousness and negative effects of territorial confrontations, you would try your best to avoid blundering into another person's territory. So if you are going into another person's department or his part of the building to do some work, and there is a chance of his behaving territorially, it is prudent to let him know in advance. Give him a call and let him know when you are going over to his area and tell him your reason for being there. If you do not call in advance, then drop by his office first and get him into the picture. If you think this is silly, then ask yourself honestly how you will feel if another department head come into your department without calling on you and appears to be settled down to work with one of your staff. Thus, silly or waste of time as it may appear, you will be surprised that if you observe this protocol the next time you see another department head's staff over some work issues, you may be saving yourself a lot of unnecessary "battles" and embarrassment arising from territorial confrontation. Much as this may surprise you, Sun Tzu is really no "war-monger" as the earlier quotation has shown. This is what Sun Tzu meant when he says:

> *Fighting to win one hundred victories in one hundred battles is not the supreme skill. To break the enemy's resistance without fighting is the supreme skill.*

This principle also applies when you have unwittingly crossed into another person's territory, resulting in his getting all "worked up" to attack (and thus repel your intrusion). The same goes if your territory is being "invaded" by others since you will be in a far more rational and unemotional frame of mind to realize that conflict can be undesirable... unless you are eagerly spoiling for a fight.

A fight is not always the best solution. As Sun Tzu has warned, war can have disastrous consequences and we need to separate our emotion from the business on hand:

> *Do not act unless in the interest of the State. Do not use your troops unless you can win. Do not fight unless you are in danger. No ruler shall put troops in the field because he is angry; no general should fight because he is resentful. For an angry man can later become happy, a resentful man become pleased*

but a kingdom once destroyed can never be restored nor the dead be brought back to life.

Prudence means always asking ourselves these three basic questions: "What are my chances of winning in a fight?" "And if I do win, what do I gain?" Finally ask, "Is the gain worth the fight?" When you have honestly answered these questions, you may realize that some fights are just not worth the effort. It is thus better to stop and think before reacting in a way we may later come to regret. So, if you had unwittingly moved into another person's territory, it is better to get out immediately and seek to repair the breach in the territorial fences by acknowledging the other person's domain over his territory unless you want a "war" on your hands.

There was an occasion when I had to get a statement urgently from the finance department. In the absence of the financial controller, I coaxed one of her staff to let me have the print-out. When I later heard the staff was reprimanded by the financial controller who was obviously displeased with my intrusion, I sought an appointment with her where I said: "I realize as you are head of finance, by right I should have got your okay before taking out the print-out as I had. But given your absence and the urgency, I was forced to demand it from your girl. Now you're back, I just have to see you personally and explain". Soft, reasonable words which go straight to the point of acknowledging her domain in her territory and humbly seeking to make amends without having to stoop to boot-licking.

I also made sure that through one of my own staff who was friendly with the accounts supervisor who was reprimanded, she learned that I had seen her boss and accepted the responsibility for "forcing" the print-out from her. Both actions ensured the subsequent goodwill between the financial controller, her staff and myself. It was simply not worth my while to fight the financial controller since my department and hers work quite closely with one another. Beside, there is nothing to be gained from fighting.

Sun Tzu has also suggested the possibility of turning disadvantages into advantages when he says:

> *Nothing is more difficult than directing maneuvers. The difficulty lies in turning the devious into the direct, and misfortune into gain. Thus, adopt an indirect route and divert the enemy by enticing him with a bait. Once done, you may march forth after he does and arrive before him. One able to do this knows the strategy of the direct and indirect.*

In this, a friend of mine, whom we shall call Augustus, has proven his expertise in the strategy of the direct and indirect. When another manager poked his head into his department and threw his car keys to one of Augustus's staff with the order to go to his car and carry a computer terminal which was urgently required by the chairman in his suite, Augustus did not put up a protest. Instead he went up to his clerk and said, "Follow me" and together they carried the terminal into the chairman's suite.

After receiving his chairman's grateful thanks, Augustus went straight to the manager's office to return the car keys and said: "Richard, thanks for getting us some credit with the old man. But I guess you were too much in a hurry for I'll appreciate even more if you'd care to check with me in future before requesting for assistance from any of my chaps. After all, they may already have some other work assignments from me and it won't be nice if they were to turn you down." The message was tactfully delivered and yet the point was taken effectively.

What about the earlier mentioned case of the two directors seeking to show their dominance in the organization? Having learned in Chapter 3, the five faults which Sun Tzu exhorts us to avoid, these two directors are obviously afflicted by the fourth fault – 'delicacy in honor causes sensitivity to shame' – and to some extent, also the third fault – 'quick temper enables you to make him look foolish.' Won't you agree that instead of looking good and powerful, they would only end up looking rather pathetic, petty and silly in their efforts to impress? In their exalted positions, they should realize respect can only be earned and not demanded. Thus, as we have seen in Chapter 4, Sun Tzu's words have come into effect in the said case:

> *Thus, the general who advances without coveting fame and withdraws without fearing disgrace, but whose sole intention is to protect the people and do good service for his ruler, is the precious jewel of the State.*

Since none of the two directors was willing to concede to the other, no decision could be reached and the vital project continued to be delayed. They were putting their self-interest before the company's. Out of frustration, several good managers subsequently left the company.

UNFAIR TACTICS

When office politicking is not well managed, the situation can really sink into a most deplorable state. As professionals, we must seek to compete fairly (not only with external competitors for the market but also with colleagues for resources, budget, positions, etc.) but in so doing, we must not be blind to unfair tactics. Earlier in Chapter 5, I have said that between an external enemy and internal dissension, the latter is more to be feared. This is because one can still come under attack from one's own side i.e. colleagues, at one's workplace. Sun Tzu says:

Seek to reduce those hostile neighboring States by inflicting harm on them. Labor them with constant trifle affairs. Lead them by their noses with superficial offers of advantages.

Although I suspect Sun Tzu was eyeing the enemies of his State when he writes this passage in his book, the implication is present even in office politicking. I must however first caution you against being carried away by what you read here but then, it is nonetheless fair that you should expect the worse instead of looking at life through rose-tinted glasses. It is my belief that as professionals, we should compete fairly albeit we must be wise to unfair tactics.

In Sun Tzu's time, inflicting harm on an enemy was through enticing away his capable staff, encouraging some to turn traitors, formenting intrigues and deceit between the enemy and his supporters, corrupting the morals of the enemy or his followers with gifts of intoxicating drugs or liquors, or lovely women so as to encourage excess and unsettling domestic harmony and official duties, etc. Today, such unscrupulous tactics vary in their usage and many young and promising executives have been led astray by heavy gambling, drugs, wine, women and song into corruption and/or failing their responsibilities which they have been entrusted. Be very careful of those who would take you to this downhill slide.

I know an elderly sales manager who felt threatened by one of his newly-hired sales executives who was quite a favorite with the customers. He subsequently led the young executive astray by introducing him to the fast life of wine, women, and songs. Once the executive was hooked and started patronizing bars and nightclubs even when not entertaining customers, the crafty sales manager steered him to those wholesalers who were known to gamble even during office hours. The sales manager told the young man: "It's our job to entertain our customers. Gambling with them is one way of making them happy and ensuring we get their orders. Besides, it is quite easy to make some money this way". He even put up a show of joining enthusiastically in the gambling session. Soon the young executive "graduated" from the dealers' afternoon sessions to the casino at Genting Highlands, which is only about an hour's drive from the Malaysian capital.

To the sales manager's delight, the young man was fast losing interest in the business – he just cannot wait for 5 p.m. when he would start to drive up to the casino to gamble until the early hours before returning home to grab a few hours' sleep and report for work looking dishevelled, distracted and tired. Needless to say, the young man was subsequently fired when it was discovered that he had been borrowing money from most of the wholesalers.

As for laboring others with trifle affairs, I once knew an assistant general manager whose favorite tactic is to assign numerous assignments of little importance (which he would insist as "urgent matters requiring immediate attention") on those managers whom he wish to get rid off. When they are busy running around attending to his "urgent matters" and neglecting their main duties, the assistant general manager would report to the chairman that so-and-so cannot handle his job. Once he felt he has got the chairman "in his pocket", he would issue show-cause letters on the unfortunate manager for the poor performance of his function. In this way, several managers who were subject to such pressure, quit the organization.

THE BOSS AND OFFICE POLITICKING

From the above, we get to see why bosses play a very important role in the management of office politics. When politicking becomes rampant and uncontrolled in the office, it is usually the fault of the boss. As Sun Tzu has observed:

When troops are inclined to flee, insubordinate against commands, distressed, disorganized or defeated, it is the fault of the general as none of these calamities arises from natural causes.

Thus, politicking in any organization if unchecked and allowed to deteriorate, can be most demoralizing to those employees who are truly committed and dedicated to the company. This is because those in power will usually covet more power and will spend their energy and thoughts towards consolidating such power and eliminating threats. Hence, they will put their self-interests before organizational ones which will even more so be in conflict with the goals of other employees. To aggravate the problem, those in power are inclined to practise favoritism by rewarding their supporters, especially in the form of placing them in jobs of responsibility and influence. Frustration and lack of job satisfaction will usually cause those employees who are not aligned to any faction to quit the organization and join others where their efforts can be accorded better recognition and be rewarded on the basis of merit.

Let us take the case of the assistant general manager mentioned earlier. He was then eyeing the general manager's job. Although he held the number 2 position in the organization, he had the chairman's support. I am thus inclined to blame the chairman for allowing politicking in the organization to get out of hand. If he had been more sincere in wanting the organization to be strong, he would have been more firm in putting a stop to the obvious politicking of the assistant general manager. The chairman's irresponsibility resulted in the mass resignation of the organization's managers – a sheer waste of human resource.

Bosses should therefore be careful in making sure that they do not allow negative politicking to start in their workplace. They should take a cue from Sun Tzu's fourth fundamental factor, 'command' which despite having been discussed earlier in Chapter 2 is yet so important that it shall be repeated here:

> *By command, I mean the general's stand for the vir-tues of wisdom, sincerity, benevolence, courage, and strictness.*

Since politic is defined as being sagacious in adopting means to an end, a wise boss should then be able to see that politicking need not necessarily be bad. It can only become bad when employees are infected by their bosses' insincerity and started behaving insincerely with one another down the hierarchy. Similarly, when bosses are petty, it will not come as a surprise to find their employees may lack benevolence in their interpersonal relationships. This is where secretaries often reflect their bosses. If one is arrogant and rude, the probability of her boss being worse is high. From experience, I found that nice secretaries usually work for nice bosses. As a boss then, have courage to stand for principles and be strict with those who try to manipulate situations to their personal and selfish advantage.

Once a manager whom I held in high esteem for his work, came up to me with a very strong complaint that his department was unable to function smoothly because of obstacles deliberately set up by another manager. He was seething with indignation and in his attack, he dropped several hints that the other manager's action could be motivated by personal interest which may be lacking in in-tegrity. After hearing him out, I got in the other manager whereupon I asked the complainant to repeat what he had told me to the "offending" manager. Needless to say, the supposedly aggrieved manager literally squirmed in his seat as he struggled unsuccessfully to diplomatize his complaint in a "...oh, well, there's this little problem...ah, misunderstand-ing..." tone.

I admit what I did was rather drastic. However, from my experience, a truly aggrieved person (i.e. one with real complaints) would be simply overjoyed that the boss not only listens but gives him a chance to clobber the offending party on the spot! It is usually those trying to play politic who would quake at the thought of having to thrash it out in front of the boss – they have no fact to back up their grouses.

To do as I did in the above situation, one must be highly skilled in manipulating both warring parties. In handling that case, I had to keep on changing masks – ranging from a stern fatherly one to show I mean business when it comes to settling the squabbles of my "wayward children", a kind, priestly one welcoming "confessions", a stern, impartial justice judging fairly the follies of men, to a caring team-leader assuring both managers that the whole exercise was not meant to pick fault and score points but as part of the team-building process. I even had to delude them into believing there was no personality clash but a need for both parties to face work problems which had arisen from the work situation. After they had amicably worked out their differences, I had a heart-to-heart talk with the manager who had tried to stab his colleague's back in the first place and counselled him on the advantages of working as a team and sharing the successes of team effort instead of sinking into bitter in-fighting which only weakens the organization. It was good that he responded well to my manipulation then. But be warned that there is no one best way to handle potential conflict situations. In another situation given other variables, I may have to use other methods as the above may just not work.

SUMMARY

This chapter looks at office politicking and accepts the fact that this phenomenon is a reality of organizational life. So long as man exist, politicking abounds and the aim of this chapter is to relate to Sun Tzu's principles in his *Art of War* to help us manage office politicking.

The important principles to remember are:

- *Realize office politic is no laughing matter* – this will ensure we will watch ourselves from stepping inadvertently into other people's territory; and if we have reasons to step into their territory, acknowledge their dominance by seeking their approval.
- A *fight may not be for the best* – ask ourselves three questions: (a) What are our chances of winning? (b) If we win, what do we get? (c) Is what we get worth the fight?
- *Make friends* – this is where coalitions in the office have been found to be a useful mean of resolving conflicts, contributing to team-building, and getting things done.
- *Gathering information* – get to know what is going on around you so that in your prepared state, you are more alert and capable of dealing with awkward situations.

All the above simply points to the principle of "breaking the enemy's resistance without actually fighting". And of course, going by Sun Tzu's principles, we should also be wise to unfair tactics such as when scheming colleagues plot to lead us astray by corrupting our morals and behavior, e.g. gambling, womanizing, alcohols, drugs, etc.

The chapter also shows why bosses play a very important role in managing office politics. A boss who fails to lead by example and who practises favoritism by favoring his supporters will cause other employees to be distressed, disobedient (from having lost respect for the insincere boss) and inclined to leave the organization. It is essential then for

113

bosses to lead by example by cultivating the five virtues – wisdom, sincerity, benevolence, courage, and strictness – which Sun Tzu has named under his fourth fundamental factor, "command".

CHAPTER 9

Management Information System

WE HAVE FINALLY come to the stage where we are about to venture forth into the external environment. At this juncture, it is wise to reflect upon Sun Tzu's famous words:

> *Therefore I say: If you know yourself and your enemy; in a hundred battles you will never fear the result. When you know yourself but not your enemy, your chances of winning or losing are equal. If you know neither yourself nor your enemy, you are certain in every battle to be in danger.*

And prior to this statement, Sun Tzu says:

Thus we may know there are five circumstances in which victory may be predicted: He who knows when he can fight and when not to fight will be victorious. He who understands the use of both large and small forces will win. He whose ranks are united in purpose will be victorious. He who is prepared and lies in wait for an enemy who is not will be victorious. He who has capable generals and without interference by the ruler will be victorious. It is in these five matters that the way to victory is known.

Hence, we should emulate Sun Tzu who must have had asked himself in those days when he was attempting to size up whether the circumstances favor him for victory. It is only with knowledge of ourselves, and knowledge – especially advanced knowledge – of our enemy that we can position ourselves according to the aforesaid circumstances. Lack of such knowledge will be disastrous for as Sun Tzu observes:

When a general fails to size up his enemy and uses inferior force to engage a larger one, or weak troops to attack the strong, or neglects to place picked men in the front ranks, the result is a rout.

Knowledge then is power. And knowledge can only come from having a good management information system. That was why the legendary Harold Geneen of ITT Corp insisted on his senior executives abiding by a two-word rule: no surprises. Executives who wanted to retain their elevated positions would have to keep him fully informed of the company's affairs, alerting him to any possible threat on the horizon before it could plunge the company into crisis.

SETTING UP AN EFFECTIVE MANAGEMENT INFORMATION SYSTEM

To set up a management information system is not really that difficult. Setting up an *effective* management information system is tougher. Effectiveness means that information must be timely, relevant and accurate.

Timeliness will ensure that the information collected and stored for use is not behind time and thus obsolete. A colleague of mine once boasted to my boss that he had compiled a fantastic database of potential clients on his department computer. When he subsequently used the data for direct-mailing, nearly 80 per cent of the mailed letters came back unopened. He later found out that his clerks were keying in names and addresses based on a 1974 directory!

For busy executives, there is only one thing worse than not having enough information, and that is having too much. I will however gladly have as much information as I can get about my competitors. Nonetheless, with the exception of information about competitors, unless you are gifted as a speed-reader with a good memory or capacity to take in as much information as possible, be discerning in your information needs. For example, when I was general manager of The Mall shopping complex, I found the following reports make essential reading:

- Marketing report showing our occupancy rate, new tenants or ongoing negotiation, market events and competitors' movement. In manufacturing and trading, such would be the sales analysis report.
- Operating budget and cashflow statement showing the plus and minuses in revenues and expenses, as well as accounts payable and receivables.

- Financial statements showing the company's up-to-date performance and position of its assets and liabilities.
- Personnel and payroll summary showing the manpower strength, employee turnover, key-employee profiles, and labor cost.
- Promotional events and advertising cost – this report is peculiar mainly to shopping complexes' and hotels' management since such establishments plan promotional events and spend on advertising such events.
- Engineering and operational reports showing the maintenance schedule and costs for running the complex, inventory, highlighting problem areas and proposing improvements to the building.

In other businesses, information needs may also include product cost report, stock status or inventory report, fixed assets' summary, R&D status and expenses, etc. Different companies in different industries have their own peculiar needs and their management information system will accordingly be set up to fulfill such needs. Hence, what is said here is meant only as a guide.

As for accuracy, it is pointless to have information which are inaccurate. In fact, inaccurate information could be more damaging than useful since it may mislead the user into making the wrong decision.

SOURCES OF INFORMATION

One shall find that the sources of information about matters external to the organisation, especially those used in compiling the abovesaid marketing report or sales analysis report are virtually unlimited. Since information is extremely vital if we are to have that competitive edge, we should try to find out as much as we can about our competitors and their activities. Such information may relate to their business plans and development, new markets, or technological break-throughs. General information about economic condition, changes in legal, political and social structure, and state of technology would also be invaluable.

Information can be acquired in a relatively cheap way, such as by subscribing to published sources. It is no wonder then that top executives spend a considerable portion of their time reading newspapers, magazines, trade journals, professional publications, etc. One of my previous bosses was rather short-sighted in this area. In attempting to cut down the company's newspaper bill, managers were arranged into groups of twos and threes to take turns and share newspapers. Just how much can one save by doing this? Beside, such practices will not only dampen executives' reading habits but will also cause them to lose interest in this essential quest for information which may be useful to the organization's survival and growth. Sun Tzu has this to say:

> *He who faces an enemy for many years to struggle for the victory that can be decided in a single day and yet remains ignorant of the enemy's position because he begrudges giving ranks, honors and a few hundred pieces of gold, is totally without humanity. Such a man is no leader, no help to his ruler, no master of victory.*

Since November 1, 1991, a comprehensive 24-hour on-line trade and business information service, GlobaLink, became available to about 2,000 companies and businessmen in Singapore. Data available to subscribers encompasses international business information covering 150 countries. This includes reports on country profiles, business trends, market intelligence, international trade procedures, trade statistics, trade opportunities customized to meet users' needs, trade directories, companies' profiles and financial statements, etc.

Information may even be obtained for free from talking to people. One reason why top executives join golf clubs is that lots of information are exchanged on the green. After all, besides swinging at the little white balls and walking miles of green searching for them, what else is there to do but talk? This is where one's network of friends and contacts is of great importance. Learn to form and cultivate your network. Sales personnel too has learned that calling on their agents, dealers, distributors, or end-users, can mean more than just sales. They can get much invaluable information from these sources about the market and the competitors.

Although somewhat more expensive but quite effective, one can get much useful information by attending conferences and seminars or directly paying a particular person or groups of persons whose profession is providing information for a fee. In today's world of corporate intelligence and security, a small coterie of professional firms are already providing such services. One of them, Kroll Associates which is the world's largest in this business, hires former employees of security or law enforcement agencies for such work which includes checking out the credentials of persons or firms which one is dealing with.

On a more direct (and somewhat confrontational approach), Sun Tzu suggests:

> *Thus, I can create victory. Even if the enemy is numerous, I can prevent him from fighting. Find out his plans to know which of his strategies will be successful and which will not. Provoke his agitation and so learn the pattern of his movement. Force him to show his disposition and so ascertain his strength and vulnerability.*

One of the ways whereby a smaller organization can provoke a larger one is by under-cutting the selling price. This may sound surprising but sometimes the big boys may find thye are unable to compete in a price war. When I was selling sugar for the Malayan Sugar Manufacturing Company Berhad in 1986, we enjoyed about 48 per cent of the Malaysian sugar market. The other 52 per cent share was shared amongst Central Sugar Refinery (25 per cent), Kilang Gula Felda Perlis (15 per cent), and Gula Padang Terap (12 per cent). One fine morning, my sources informed me that one of the agents for Gula Padang Terap was selling at a "give away" discount of RM2.00 per 50-kg bag. Since sugar is a fast-moving consumer item, the profit margin is very low and we, at Malayan Sugar were then giving only RM1.00 discount on average to our wholesalers. Needless to say, the telephone calls started coming in a few days later when our wholesalers found out about the RM2.00 discount and pressed us for more discounts.

We were then selling close to 1,000 tons a day as compared to Gula Padang Terap's 250 tons. And if we had allowed ourselves to be easily provoked and got caught in a price war by matching their discounts, then for a one-year period, it would have cost us a hefty RM14.6 million as compared to a paltry RM3.65 million of Gula Padang Terap! Although we could financially absorb this cost, from the information we got about Gula Padang Terap's capacity being restricted to only 250 tons a day and even then, only for a limited period of time since production is dependant on local plantation harvest instead of raw sugar import, we felt it would be unnecessary and unwise to be caught in a price war. We chose then to adopt a different strategy, i.e. channelling attention to our product quality and reliability of delivery. For example, we reminded our dealers how we stood by them during the sugar shortage when other refineries were unable to meet their needs.

While people in business tends not to be openly confrontational, they are nonetheless not unknown to engage in covert activities to find out more about their competitors and their businesses. This is the area commonly referred to as industrial espionage. Banish all thoughts of cloak-and-dagger mysteries, James Bond look-alikes or the misconception that only the morally ambiguous persons resort to using spies. Although some people have condemned such activities as underhand, illegal and immoral, my personal feeling is that all is fair in war. I have often found the same persons resorting to such means when it suits their purpose. So I will not pretend to be holier-than-thou for otherwise I shall have to forget altogether about this chapter.

Sun Tzu has this to say about espionage:

> *The enlightened ruler and the wise general can subdue the enemy whenever they move and they can achieve superhuman feats because they have foreknowledge. This foreknowledge cannot be obtained from spirits, gods, nor by reasoning over past events, nor by calculations. It can only be obtained from men who know the enemy position.*

The following shows some of the ways how one can overtly or covertly obtain information from "men who know the enemy position":

1. *Milking Potential Recruits* – In the past when conducting job interviews, I found some applicants who were then working for competitors openly telling me about whatever was happening in their organizations. In response to my questions on the nature of their work, their achievements, etc., they would often unknowingly or even deliberately become invaluable sources of information. A few even volunteered to gather and bring over information which could benefit us. Of course, they would be subsequently employed but they could never really be trusted even though some may be genuinely discontented with working for their previous employers. The point here is that if they can

"sell out" their bosses, they will do the same to me another day.

2. *Conducting Phony Job Interviews* – This is an even more deliberate activity than the one described above. Here, the intention is not really to employ but rather to get the selected "candidates" to talk and hopefully reveal some useful information pertaining to their organizations.

3. *Hiring People Away From Competitors* – There is a slight difference here when compared to the earlier-mentioned attempt to milk potential recruits. First, it is a deliberate "head-hunting" activity. As Sun Tzu has suggested:

> *Whichever army you wish to attack, cities you wish to conquer, people you wish to assassinate, you must know the names of the commanders, chief assistants, bodyguards, sentries and other subordinates, so make your spies check and acquire these facts accurately.*

I am an avid reader of newspapers and magazines not only to monitor events but also to find out more about people and their background and file away such information for future use. Sometimes certain persons are featured in the news and I will have my secretary cut out the news items for compilation into personal dossiers. In this way, I may get to identify key people, understand their individual personality, style of operation and favorite tactics. In the event that they may be useful to my organization, I shall have them "head-hunted".

Second, these persons may be accorded more trust than those described in (1) above because they did not offer to turn over information in the first place. Instead we are the ones who made the initial move to convert them by appealing to their sense of challenge, better prospects, etc.

4. *Deliberately Planting Spies In Competitors' Firms* – There have been cases where a person leaves his organization to join a competitor for a while before returning to his original organization. Some of these people may even be deliberately planted in the competitors' firms. There is one case I know where the "spy-master" even went to the extent of getting his nephew to apply and join his rival's firm. His rationale was that his competitors would be more inclined to employ and trust his nephew since the latter was not employed by him and thus there was no apparent link between them.

5. *Encouraging Key Customers To Talk* – From my experience, key customers such as my wholesalers and industrial buyers are always more than ready to talk given the slightest encouragement. They will talk and talk... But do not take everything they say as the Gospel truth. As Sun Tzu has advised:

> *Only the one who is wise and sagely, benevolent and just, can use secret agents. Only he who is sensitive and subtle can get the truth of their reports.*

The key here is getting the truth out of their reports. I have found that most key customers, especially wholesalers, are motivated by personal gains ("How will this benefit me?") and their information will contain both truths and half-truths, sprinkled with some outright lies. You must be perceptive enough to sort these out.

6. *Interviewing Competitors* – While we may not do this directly, we may still be able to do it indirectly, i.e. via other people. As Sun Tzu has said:

    Generally, in battle, use the direct method to engage the enemy's forces; indirect methods however are needed to secure victory.

    There was this chief executive I used to do business with. He was on very good terms with a journalist. And knowing his rival has a huge ego for publicity, he "leaked" to his journalist friend that there was a good story to be had from the rival. When the journalist got onto his rival, sure enough the rival grabbed at the bait and gave an exclusive interview where he talked and talked... with the results that my chief executive friend got what he wanted to know. The lesson to learn here is that it is not wrong to grab whatever publicity you can for your organization BUT be careful with what you are going to say. Tell the press only the "open" secret – things that everyone already knew.

    Another way of interviewing your competitors is getting someone to pose as potential customer or supplier. Although far more risky, it is nonetheless practised by some people.

7. *Taking Plant Tours* – Although organizations are usually reluctant to allow visitors from known rivals to visit their plants, they sometimes make exception in the case of visitors from organiza-

tions not directly in competition. This is even more true of formal exchanges between countries. Highly trained and observant engineers have been known to take in what they see and reproduce blueprint after visiting their hosts' plants. But since they would usually be shown only where their hosts would allow them to go, this method will not give a total picture. A friend recently told me how some Japanese visitors to an American plant were shortly after the visit able to produce materials bearing chemical components which were exact in specifications. Although they were searched on exit, unknown to the gate security personnel, these visitors were wearing shoes whose specially-made adhesive soles glued on the materials' scrap on the floor besides the machinery.

8. *Taking Competitors' Products Apart* – It is common knowledge that the Japanese are experts in this area. Western industrialists would spend years and fortunes in research and development activities. But the moment they put a product in the market, the Japanese would buy it, take it apart, improve on it, and hey presto, there is a new and better product in the market and all at minimal cost since little R&D is incurred. Such clever acts of technology pilferage have caused some embarrassment to the Japanese, for example the 1988 incident whereby the American Arbitration Association ordered Fujitsu Limited to pay US$237 million to the International Business Machines Corporation for pilfering its software programmes.

9. *Buying Competitors Garbage* – Executives are known to scribble notes, crumple the paper and then chuck it into the office waste-paper basket. Secretaries are also known to throw out documents – either thought to be obsolete or extras (thanks to photocopiers) – into waste-paper baskets. Knowing such activities are daily occurrences in the office, industrial spies are known to have bought garbage from the collectors and thereafter playing the "jigsaw-puzzle" game of piecing scraps of documents and attempting to figure out what is going on. A disgusting business but high returns for the enemy if one is not too careful with what one throws into the waste-paper baskets. This is why someone has invented such machines called paper "shredders" nowadays.

COUNTER-INTELLIGENCE

In the following passage of Sun Tzu, the importance of information is once again emphasized:

> *By discovering my enemy's dispositions and at the same time concealing mine from him, I can concentrate my forces while he must divide his forces. Knowing his dispositions, I can use my total strength against a part of his. If he is ignorant of mine, he will have to spread out his forces to defend every point. This will give me superiority in numbers. And if I were to use my superior strength to attack an inferior one, those I deal with will be in dire straits. The enemy must not know where I intend to attack. For if he knows not, he must prepare for possible attack in many places; and in such*

preparation, his forces shall be so spread out that those I have to fight at any given point will be few.

Once we know what our competitors are up to, and without their knowing what we are up to, we will be in a superior position to control the situation. This is what most strategists mean by what they have described as having the competitive edge. It is in this way that our customers' base may be expanded or our penetration into competitors' market be made without alerting them into taking preventive measures against us. We shall discuss this in some details later in Chapter 11 when touching on strategy formulation.

But what we can do to competitors, remember that they too can do the same to us. That is why Sun Tzu advises:

The supreme skill in commanding troops is in the shapeless command. Then the prying of the subtlest spies cannot penetrate for the laying of plans against you. The shapes I take shall lay plans for victory but such are beyond the comprehension of the masses. While all can see the external aspects, none can understand the way I scored my victory.

The fundamental rule to remember in information security and counter-intelligence is the "need-to-know" principle. Information flow should preferably be a one-way flow, i.e. upwards from all levels of the hierarchy to end up in top management's custody. In this way, facts gathered could be analyzed and secrets would be kept at the top-most level and be made accessible only to those on a "need-to-know" basis. That is why Sun Tzu has been rather insistent that:

He [the general] must be capable of mystifying his officers and men so that they are in ignorance of his true intention.

also,

Assign tasks to your soldiers without detailing your plan. Show them the advantages without revealing the dangers.

So be discreet. While we may seek to learn about our competitors, we must be careful about their learning about us. Be close-mouthed and alert to the following situations which may result in leakage of information.

1. *Indiscretion In The Office* – Some organizations have a system whereby visitors are entertained in a common lounge or meeting rooms instead of being allowed to wander about the offices. If your organization do not have such a system, then train your staff to be careful about what documents they leave about on their desk.

   Shortly after my promotion as general manager of The Mall, the manager of a rival complex paid me a courtesy visit to "congratulate" me. Although I appreciate the goodwill and look forward to closer cooperation between our companies, I was also suspicious of other motive besides plain old-fashioned courtesy. Before receiving him in my room, I placed a pre-typed marketing report giving misleading rates and figures on my desk. I arranged for other non-important files to cover that fake report but with the report jutting out conspicuously and showing its title. Shortly after he was in my room, I excused myself to go to the washroom for a few minutes. When I returned, I observed the files had been disturbed. Had I been careless and the report was a genuine one, it would have been bad for my company. While I wish the said gentleman could be reading this book, I must hasten to remind, "All's Fair In War".

When entertaining visitors, one should also avoid taking business calls over the telephone. I have seen some executives who were so engrossed in their calls that they forgot all about their visitors whose ears (i.e. mine) were busy.

Although this can be difficult, our employees should nonetheless be encouraged to exercise more discretion over what they say to each other in the office. There is a difference in cooperative pooling of information and talking out of hand. While the former is necessary for furthering the work effort, the latter is totally unnecessary.

2. *Indiscretion In The Lifts Or Office Cafeteria* – Also train your staff not to talk shop while riding the office lifts. I know a sales manager who every now and then would send his staff to his competitor's building to ride the lifts up and down during the lunch hour for the purpose of picking up loose talk. The cafeteria of office buildings is another place where I have often overheard executives or secretaries sitting at nearby tables talking shop.

3. *Indiscretion When Chauffeur-driven* – If you are a big boss who enjoys the use of a company car and chauffeur, be discreet when you are being driven around by your chauffeur. I met a chauffeur once who told me most interesting stories about his boss's business as well as private life. Whether your travelling companions are company's visitors, colleagues, friends or immediate family, no shop talk. And if you are using the car-phone while being chauffeur-driven, listen more than talk. If you must talk, be alert and phrase your sentences as discreetly as possible.

4. *Indiscretion At The Golf Club* – We have been told that deals are often made while swinging at little white balls over large expanse of green. But what we have not been told is that secrets are often likely to be heard and subsequently repeated when the services of caddies are used. On the other hand, some top managers I know swear there is no safer place on earth to tell another person a secret than at the golfing green. This may be true but make sure only the ones whose ears the secret is intended for are present.

5. *Indiscretion At Home* – Home, sweet, home. In my first book, *War At Work* I mentioned how I once explained to my wife when she complained that I have not been attentive to the way she looks or dresses: such details would normally not have escaped my attention at the workplace as my senses are finely honed to watch out for anything out of the norm, but at home, well, I feel safe... I am no more at war and therefore I can afford to let my guard down. It is this relaxed feeling that causes many people to talk freely about their work at home. Such information may innocently pass on over the mahjong table or cups of tea when the spouses socialize with their friends. While I believe that people should nurture an open relationship with their spouses, they should nonetheless exercise discretion when it comes to their corporate matters which require extreme confidence.

6. *Alert To Planted Spies* – Last but not least, take note of the following exhortation by Sun Tzu:

> *It is important to find out who are those*
> *sent by the enemy to spy on you, and bribe*
> *them to serve you instead. Tempt them with*
> *bribes and house them well. This way you*
> *not only convert them for your use but also*
> *get to recruit other agents...*

This means two can always play the same game. If you can see through any would-be spies seeking to infiltrate your organization, you may still use them. If they are useful to you, then seek to turn them around by treating them kindly, psychologically influencing them to your cause, and reinforcing such influence by rewarding them generously with good jobs, high salary, etc. On the other hand, if they are not so useful to be turned around, feed them with wrong information and thus mislead whoever sends them in the first place. Sun Tzu calls this later category, converted spies, for he says:

> *Converted spies are really the enemy's spies*
> *whom we feed with false information or*
> *make use of to spread rumors so as to lure*
> *the enemy into our traps.*

Who says this is a pleasant world? But then, warfare has never been pleasant. Business is war ... and "All Is Fair In War".

SUMMARY

In this chapter, we are again reminded that it is with knowledge of ourselves, and knowledge – especially advanced knowledge – of our enemy that we can control the circumstances for victory and avoid disastrous consequences in our ventures. Knowledge then is power. And knowledge can only come from having a good management information system.

To set up a management information system is not really that difficult. Setting up an effective management information system is tougher because to be effective, information must be timely, relevant and accurate. Timeliness will ensure that the information collected and stored for use is not behind time and thus obsolete. Relevance means one has to be discerning in information search since information must be appropriate for the purpose for which it is required. As for accuracy, it is essential because it would not only be pointless but also damaging to have information which are inaccurate.

Some examples of essential reports are given though it is stressed that different companies in different industries have their own peculiar needs and their management information system will accordingly be set up to fulfill such needs.

The reader is also shown how he could acquire information whose sources are virtually unlimited. For example, information can be acquired in a relatively cheap way, such as by subscribing to published sources, like newspapers, magazines, trade journals, professional publications, etc., or to the 24-hour on-line trade and business information service, GlobaLink. Information may even be obtained for free from talking to people through one's network of friends and contacts. Sales personnel can also source information about the market and competitors from their agents, dealers, distributors, or end-users. Although somewhat more expensive but quite effective, one can get much useful information by attending conferences and seminars or directly paying a particular person or groups of persons whose profession is providing information for a fee.

Putting aside issues such as fair play, legality, and morality, other potential sources of information include milking potential recruits; conducting phony job interviews;

hiring people away from competitors; deliberately planting spies in competitors' firms; encouraging key customers to talk; interviewing competitors; taking plant tours; taking competitors' products apart; and buying competitors garbage.

The objective is to obtain the competitive edge. But what we can do to competitors, remember that they too can do the same to us. Some suggestions of how to maintain information security and counter espionage are that we must be close-mouthed and alert to indiscretion which may result in leakage of information. Examples are given of indiscretion in the office; in the lifts or office cafeteria; when being chauffeur-driven; at the golfing green or at home. It was further suggested that we should be alert to planted spies. If we can see through any would-be spies seeking to infiltrate our organization, we may either seek to turn them around by treating them kindly and through psychological influence; or feed them with wrong information and thus mislead whoever sends them in the first place.

PART IV

Managing The External Environment

CHANGE

According to Sun Tzu, "If one seeks to be victorious, he must, 'modify his tactics according to the enemy situation'." This means one must be capable of anticipating and adapting to changing circumstances.

CHAPTER 10

The Strategy Formulation Process

WE NOW COME to the part of this book where we shall seek to use the knowledge already acquired of ourselves and our immediate operating environment to move on to know and manage the external environment. This is where we shall attempt to formulate strategy that is more suitable and effective for our respective organizations.

Five stages are involved in strategy formulation:

1. Determine the corporate mission;
2. Appraise the organization;
3. Appraise the environment;
4. Set objective; and
5. Decide on the strategy to use.

MISSION DETERMINATION

As we have already seen very early in Chapter 2, mission is what Sun Tzu in his time, has called the 'moral factor' and refers to an organization's continuing purposes with regard to certain categories of persons, i.e. what is to be accomplished for whom? There are missions for customers, employees, shareholders, etc.

For example, one of the factors which has attracted me to join Kentucky Fried Chicken (KFC) is its mission statement: "Our mission is to maintain and enhance our position as the leading Western Quick Service Restaurant chain serving good value, innovative chicken-based products away from home through consistently providing a pleasant dining experience with fast, friendly service at clean and convenient locations. At all times, we must be dedicated to providing excellent service and delighting customers". This mission is further reinforced by KFC's value statement in that the company recognizes and respects the contributions of each employee, is committed to staff training and development, believes in teamwork, and respects different opinions. It would be unthinkable for me to work in an organization whose cause I do not personally subscribe to. However, be forewarned that like all things, mission and value statements may be mere words, or they may change. Thus, when the Inno-Pacific group in Singapore divested its 50 per cent shareholding in late 1992 to the other shareholder, KFC-International, the inevitable changes brought about by the latter throughout 1993 led to my leaving KFC in early 1994 in search of a more conducive environment and whose cause I can believe.

Similarly, GM's mission statement on its employees is most explicit in declaring the company as one which "practises progressive people-centred management". It went on to announce: "A company always committed to the highest standard of staff training and development, providing ample challenges within a positive working environment". In all its recruitment advertisement, GM further advertises itself as the employer who cares. To back this declaration, it has even employed a manager specifically to look after employees' compensation and benefits.

We have also seen Sun Tzu's stand:

> *By moral law, I mean that which causes the people to be in total accord with the ruler, so that they will follow him in life and unto death without fear for their lives and undaunted by any peril.*

It is fundamental then for organizations to have missions. Companies usually start out with a single mission, i.e., for the purpose of serving the owners. Shareholders expect a return on their investment and thus look to dividends and capital gains from increased share values. Such returns are expected to have a higher return than prevailing interest rates in view of the higher risks involved. But to achieve this purpose, companies must also fulfill other purposes to other groups of persons, such as employees (as we have seen from the corporate philosophy of GM earlier) who expect favorable benefits and treatment in return for their effort and customers who expect quality products and value for money, etc.

APPRAISING THE ORGANIZATION AND THE ENVIRONMENT

This activity is greatly dependent on the extent of effectiveness of our management information system. This is why I have stressed the importance of having a good information system in the previous chapter. On the assumption that we have a reliably sound system, it pays at this stage to recall Sun Tzu's Seven Elements where he asks:

- Which ruler possesses the moral law?
- Whose commander has the most ability?

- Which army obtains the advantages of heaven and earth?
- On which side are regulations and instructions better carried out?
- Which army is the stronger?
- Which has the better-trained officers and men; and
- In which army is there certainty for rewards and punishment being dispensed?

Just as Sun Tzu in his times, asked the above questions in an attempt to evaluate how his army would compare against that of his enemy, we also appraise our organization and the environment by asking questions.

We can turn to the following commonly-used tools:

1. Internal analysis (or functional audit) which we have already discussed in Chapter 7. This tool is mainly for appraising an Organization's functional areas;

2. S-W-O-T (the acronym for Strengths-Weaknesses-Opportunities-Threats) analysis. Also called WOTS-UP, this tool can be used to appraise both the internal organization as well as the external environment;

3. Environmental Scan.

Using S-W-O-T Analysis

S-W-O-T stands for strengths, weaknesses, opportunities, and threats. We have thus been given a framework (see S-W-O-T Matrix in Figure 2) whereby to identify these factors and thereafter group them accordingly. The framework helps us to see our position more clearly and thereby allows us to analyze the given factors and plan our next moves. We shall now look at each of the individual factors:

Figure 2
S-W-O-T Matrix

MY STRENGTHS	MY WEAKNESSES
1.	1.
2.	2.
3.	3.
4.	4.
5.	5.
THREATS (My Rival's Strengths)	OPPORTUNITIES (My Rival's Weaknesses)
1.	1.
2.	2.
3.	3.
4.	4.
5.	5.
ACTION PLAN	
1.	
2.	
3.	

1. *Strengths refer to the internal competencies which an organization has, in comparison with its competitors* – Kodak's strength lies in the easy availability of its little yellow box. You need not have to go only to photoshops to pick up a roll of Kodak photographic film. You can pick one up even at the neighborhood's drugstore, newspaper stand, candy store, petrol stations or

supermarket. No wonder then that when most people think of photographic film, they think of Kodak. In the USA alone, there are about 200,000 Kodak film outlets representing some 85 per cent of the market share. Besides, its instruction sheet is printed in eight languages which has made it a global name.

Volvo cars sell on its strength – safety. Its "steel-cage" structure which is further backed by anti-lock brakes, front seat pre-tensioning seat-belts and a new center position 3-point seat-belt in the rear, is a great attraction for the safety-conscious motorists. In the case of another automaker, Volkswagen, its strength was in the small size of its Beetle. But when flushed with the success of having had captured 67 per cent of the imported car market in the USA, it started thinking big by churning out in rapid succession, the 8-passenger Wagon, the 4-door 411 and 412 sedans, the sporty Dasher, and the "Thing" jeep. Its advertisements switched from "Think Small" to "Different Volks for different folks". As a result, its market share plummeted to less than 7 per cent of the imported market.

2. *Weaknesses refer to the organization's attributes which decrease its competence in comparison with competitors* – As we have just seen, Volkswagen weakness surfaced when it tried to encroach the market of big, good-looking cars which has all the while been dominated by General Motors. When Volkswagen brought in the Beetle, General Motors was stumped – they did not know how to handle the situation. A small car against their big ones, an ugly car against their good-looking ones, a car whose engine is in the

wrong place – in the rear which should be the boot! Everything is unexpected and just not right. Volkswagen's strategy fits with Sun Tzu's exhortation:

> ...*move by unexpected routes and attack where he has made no defence.*

But the day Volkswagen tried to play the same game as General Motors – making big, good-looking cars – the latter was no longer stumped. That is their turf where they can always run rings round Volkswagen.

3. *Threats refer to a reasonably probable event which, if it were to occur, would be damaging to the organization* – When I was with Magnum Corporation Berhad, I discovered that the few companies in the gaming (a less embarrassing word for gambling) business would constantly be on the alert for any change in the Government stand towards gaming. Given that Malaysia is an Islamic country, we could never be sure when gaming would be banned. Hence, Genting Berhad which operates the country's only casino, has over the years sought to lessen the impact of such an event by developing its land in Genting Highlands into a hotel-resort with good entertainment facilities and golf club as well as investing overseas, notably in Australia. In 1988, Magnum too tried to diversify into property development. Sports Toto has moved into manufacturing and trading. You can imagine then the jitters in the industry when the Minister of Social Welfare announced the Government's decision to cease the Government-run lottery game in 1989.

4. *Opportunities could be seen as a combination of events, time, and place which is likely to benefit an organization which is capable of taking some courses of action accordingly* – Jogging and tennis have become increasingly popular. And when footwear importer Robert Gamm went jogging or played tennis, he found he had a problem putting away his car keys and loose change. This inconvenience caused him to see an opportunity which led to his introducing the Kanga-Roos athletic shoes with a zippered pocket on the side. Needless to say, sales hit almost US$75 million a year.

Strengths and weaknesses as found in oneself and, the internal environment, should be compared against those of the enemy. In conjunction with Sun Tzu's Seven Elements, the following five applies:

- Whose commander has the most ability?
- On which side are regulations and instructions better carried out?
- Which army is the stronger?
- Which has the better-trained officers and men; and
- In which army is there certainty for rewards and punishment being dispensed?

Opportunities and threats on the other hand are mainly influenced by the external environment and against Sun Tzu's Seven Elements, the following two applies:

- Which ruler possesses the moral law?
- Which army obtains the advantages of heaven and earth?

S-W-O-T analysis can also be used to sort out our personal problems. For example, after completing my MBA, I returned to Singapore where I have decided to settle down. While searching for a job, I listed down my strengths, weaknesses, opportunities and threats.

My strengths are my then 12 years-plus of experience in commerce and industry, especially my forte in "people" management, and my added qualification of an MBA degree. As far as I could see, my weaknesses are that I am not a local and this may discourage potential employers from taking me on given the "red tape" involved in seeking approval from the Immigration Department. Besides, my strength is also my weakness: having been a general manager for some 15 months, even though I accomplished many objectives for my company, I would still be regarded with some doubts by potential employers if I were to apply for general manager's position. On the other hand, if I were to apply for a functional manager's post, say, in human resource management, those general managers interviewing me would certainly wonder why having had been a general manager, I would now "condescend" to being only a functional manager (this is the ego viewpoint), or whether I could accept the "lower" job (again the ego viewpoint), or worse whether I would become a threat (the insecurity viewpoint) to them.

Daily job advertisements show there are plenty of opportunities in Singapore yet for all my applications, I found no taker. The threat that is always looming in the horizon is that once the island-republic is overcrowded with

Hong Kong migrants fleeing 1997, the Singapore Government may soon change its mind about welcoming graduates and professionals – all the more reason why I then needed to get a job fast and qualify for permanent residence status.

Once my position was clarified, my direction became clearer. Instead of going for general management and functional management positions, I opted for management consultancy or to return to commerce and industry in a divisional management position.

Using Environmental Scanning

This is a two-step technique which involves:

1. Gathering of information on:

   - the economic, political and social structure of the countries we operate in;
   - markets which supply the raw materials and buy the finished products;
   - competitors' behavior;
   - state of technology of the particular industry and the complementary ones.

2. Evaluation of information gathered by relating the organization to its environment.

   As an illustration, let me share with you what a hotelier friend has told me as to some of the likely questions his top management team would be asking when utilizing this tool to formulate their strategic plan:

   - What is the state of the national economy in terms of present and anticipated growth, the number of tourists arriving, their length of stay, their spending behavior *vis-a-vis* the currency exchange?

- How would their hotel compare to their closest competitor in terms of the number of rooms and room-nights booked, the occupancy rates, the room rates, revenue of each profit centre, expenditure for staff, marketing, public relations, food and beverages, etc., profit levels, staff/guest ratio, recruitment, training and labor turnover?

- Are there any new hotel opening, and if so, how are they positioned in terms of number of rooms, room rates, staff/guest ratio, etc?

SETTING OBJECTIVE

This step specifies the corporate-level objective or direction. I would differentiate objective from mission in that objective is the means by which to fulfill the corporate mission. As Sun Tzu has so simply put it:

Victory is the main objective in war.

The name of the game is winning. After all, he did win in all his five campaigns against the State of Chu by destroying the Chu's capital, Ying-du, causing King Zhao to flee, and for the next 20 years, he never lost in any battle. In meeting this objective of winning war, Sun Tzu had fulfilled his mission:

...the general who understands war is the arbiter of the people's fate and on him depends whether the nation shall be at peace or in danger.

147

A State needs to be at peace and free from danger. Likewise, in the business world, if not for the common objective of productivity which results in profitability, how else can employees enjoy job security (or lifetime employment as some of the more established Japanese organizations have practised), customers have their needs satisfied, suppliers get business and prompt payments, shareholders get their returns on investments, etc?

Objective however means different things to different people or organizations. Let us take the four main automobile companies in the USA – General Motors, Ford, Chrysler, and American Motors – to illustrate this point. As the largest, General Motors will be happy in continuing to be number one. If Ford can increase its market share, no matter how slightly, it will represent a substantial victory. For Chrysler, I believe Lee Iacocca will smile if the company can survive profitably. As for American Motors, being the smallest with only 2 per cent of the market, survival would be good enough.

Two essential characteristics of objectives which must be borne in mind are:

- Objectives must be challenging yet attainable;
- Objectives must be specific.

FORMULATING STRATEGY

Given the importance and vast scope of this subject, it shall be discussed separately in the next chapter.

SUMMARY

In this chapter, we utilize the knowledge already acquired of ourselves and our immediate operating environment to know and manage the external environment. At this stage, the intention is to formulate strategy that is more suitable and effective for our respective organizations.

Five stages in strategy formulation – mission determination; organization appraisal; environment appraisal; objective setting; and strategy choice – are discussed. It is found that organizations need to have missions which are regarded as continuing purposes for their existence. The appraisal of both the organization and the environment is greatly dependent on the extent of effectiveness of one's management information system.

The reader is also shown two tools commonly used in appraising organization – internal analysis (or functional audit) used for appraising an organization's functional areas; and S-W-O-T (acronym for Strengths-Weaknesses-Opportunities-Threats) analysis which is also called WOTS-UP. The latter, together with the technique called environmental scan, could also be deployed in appraising the external environment.

Through S-W-O-T, we find a framework (see Figure 2 – page 141) whereby to identify the factors of strengths, weaknesses, opportunities and threats and thereafter group them accordingly. The framework helps us to see our position more clearly and thereby allows us to analyze the given factors and plan our next moves. Strengths and weaknesses are apparent in oneself, the internal environment, and in comparison with those of the enemy while opportunities and threats are mainly influenced by the external environment. We also see how S-W-O-T analysis can be used to sort out our personal lives.

Environmental scan is a two-step technique. First, it gathers information on economic, political and social structure of the countries we operate in; the markets which supply the raw materials and buy the finished products; competitors' behavior; and the state of technology of the particular industry as well as complementary ones. Next, it evaluates the information gathered by relating the organization to its environment.

Objective setting specifies the corporate-level objective or direction. Two essential characteristics of objectives are that:

- objectives must be challenging yet attainable; and
- they must be specific.

Given the importance and vast scope of this subject, strategy formulation is to be discussed separately in more details in the next chapter.

GROWTH

This character signifies "life"
or "living" which means the
objective of strategy formulation
is to enable the organization to
grow or survive. Without
strategies, no growth can be
sustained.

CHAPTER 11

Formulating Strategy

THERE ARE MANY kinds of strategies which a person can utilize to compete with his competitors in business. The entire year that I was reading for my MBA, I was surprised my ear-drums managed to survive the continuous onslaught from my professors whose one-track minds seemed to be preoccupied with nothing else except market penetration, market development, product development, diversification, etc. Talk of Sun Tzu and his grandiose expressions, modern-day academicians are just as bad albeit using modern terminology. The following are some common marketing strategies in use, and for the sake of the uninitiated, they can be briefly explained as:

- *Market Penetration* – going after competitor's market shares with the same products or services;

- *Market Development* – entering new markets with existing products or services;
- *Product Development* – developing new products or services for the existing markets;
- *Diversification* – developing new products or services for new markets.

Since we are looking at strategies from the viewpoint of Sun Tzu's *Art of War*, we can conveniently categorize them under these three main groups:

1. Defensive Strategy;
2. Overtly Offensive Strategy;
3. Covertly Offensive Strategy.

The choice of whichever strategy to adopt depends on the following factors:

- Is it worthwhile to fight?
- Are you strong enough to fight?
- Even if you are strong enough to fight, are you yet weak in your defence?
- Are you left without any choice but to fight?

IS IT WORTHWHILE TO FIGHT?

Sun Tzu has much to say on the topic:

> *One who does not thoroughly understand the calamity of war shall be unable to thoroughly comprehend the advantage of war.*

and,

> *Move only if there is a real advantage to be gained...*

as well as,

> *Do not fight unless in the interest of the State... move when there is benefit to gain...*

From the above passages, we find that those who perceived Sun Tzu to be a war-monger could never be further from the truth. Although he was a brilliant military strategist and campaigner, he has shown a compassionate understanding of the horrors of war. In business, executives should therefore emulate him by taking their responsibility to their organizations seriously and temper their inherent aggression. Some fights are just not worth it. So be careful of plunging into a full-scale marketing war that may be prolonged and wasteful of resources. By such aggression, we will not really be doing any good for our organization. Therefore, think twice before you draw up a marketing plan advocating "attack-attack-attack" as if your competitor will merely stand still and do nothing in retaliation.

ARE YOU STRONG ENOUGH TO FIGHT?

Sun Tzu has made this observation:

> *The way of fighting is that: if our force is ten times the enemy's, then surround him; five times his, attack him; if double his strength, divide our force into two and use as 'alternate strategy'; if only equal to his, we must concentrate our force to fight him...if our force is so much weaker than the enemy's, we should totally avoid him...*

This explains why it is always better to avoid attacking a competitor where he is strong. A classic example is BMW's attempt to take on Mercedes Benz. As the latter arrived first in the market, it has preempted the engineering position. Since BMW's "ultimate driving machine" appeals to the younger drivers as it is newer and less expensive, it should avoid trying to better Mercedes in terms of engineering – it would be a sheer waste of effort and resources. One shall fight only if one is strong enough and the prize is worth the effort. Attack when the enemy is most vulnerable. It was such a situation which enabled the British conglomerate, Grand Metropolitan to make a successful takeover bid for the Pillsbury Company in late 1988. Pillsbury had already been through three CEO's changes in two years, suffering low returns on its equity, and having franchisees of its largest subsidiary, Burger King, mutinying over its over-capitalization. As a result, it was unable to secure a bank loan and lure any friendly "suitors" which made it most vulnerable to Grand Metropolitan's bid. Besides, Sun Tzu also observes:

> *An army cannot fight without equipment, food, or stores.*

This means we must be sure we have more than enough of each of the basic four M's – money, manpower, machinery and materials.

EVEN IF YOU ARE STRONG ENOUGH TO FIGHT, ARE YOU YET WEAK IN YOUR DEFENCE?

Sun Tzu has this to say:

> *Defends when one's strength is insufficient; attacks when abundant.*

and,

> *If I know my soldiers are capable of attacking the enemy but unaware that he is invulnerable to attack, my chance of victory is but half...if I know he can be attacked and my soldiers are capable of doing it but are unaware that the terrain is unsuited for fighting, I should hold back for my chance of victory is but half.*

Such a situation can occur when one has insufficient knowledge of the market or the market is too volatile and changeable for anyone to pin it down for any given period of time. Sometimes, a market instability could arise from rapid technological changes. Besides, for one who is strong enough to attack his competitor, he must further ask himself whether he could sustain a counter-attack or more likely, an attack from a third party waiting at the side lines to jump into the fight. It is just pointless to go on the offensive when one's defence is yet inadequate.

ARE YOU LEFT WITHOUT ANY CHOICE BUT TO FIGHT?

According to Sun Tzu:

> *Do not fight unless you are in danger.*

Hence, try not to pick a fight with a much smaller organization unless your failure to wipe it off the map altogether at this point will mean disastrous consequences for you later on. It can be quite tempting sometimes to prey on the weak rather than take on the strong. But these small firms could also be avid readers of Sun Tzu's work and thus smitten by the above exhortation.

Even if they are no Sun Tzu's followers, it has been found to be true that the smaller the organization, the harder it will fight to protect whatever little it has got. It will throw in just everything – price cuts, discounts, longer warranties or credit period. After all, remember, it has nothing to lose. As Sun Tzu has said and it is wise to bear this in mind:

> *One who has few must prepare for defence; one who has many shall make the enemy prepare for defence.*

In this way, even if you have no option, do not despair. If you know the *Art of War*, then, you can still make the best of your situation.

DEFENSIVE STRATEGY

Defensive warfare should not be taken to mean a passive acceptance of one's weaker position in the face of stronger rivals. Sometimes leading companies will also take a defensive stance to protect what they have already got. Thus, good defence should be seen as offensive in nature with the clear objective of protecting one's market share. As such, those seeking to defend should do well to remember a fundamental principle which Sun Tzu has advocated:

> It is a principle of war that we do not assume the enemy will not come, but instead we must be prepared for his coming; not to presume he will not attack, but instead to make our own position unassailable.

Defensive strategy does not call for one to be reactive in nature. Instead, it should be viewed as a proactive exercise. That is why Sun Tzu has said:

> Skilful warriors of ancient times first sought for themselves an invincible position whereby to await the opportunity to get at their enemy's vulnerability.

You must thus build strengths from your weaknesses. As we have already seen in Chapter 3 when seeking to build one's personal strengths, this sort of activity requires much self-discipline:

> The good commander seeks virtues and goes about disciplining himself according to the laws so as to effect control over his success.

The same principle applies here except that we are now considering the organization as a whole instead of only our personal selves. For companies to be disciplined and honest with themselves means being able to "attack" themselves. Attacking themselves means having the guts to chop off products which are not doing well or to replace those which are about to enter the decline phase as depicted on the product life cycle (see Figure 1 – page 17). A good example is the International Business Machines Corporation, better known as IBM. It does not wait for its existing products to become obsolete but every now and then will introduce a new line of mainframe computers which gives significant improvements in both price and performance. By this move, the company could ensure that competitors are always lagging behind.

And while you are seeking to make improvements over your weaknesses, you should at the same time be watching your competitors keenly and monitoring their every movement in the market. Even companies which are already entrenched in their business should not relax their vigilance in ensuring their share of the market. Thus, although IBM has proven its capability to attack itself, it made one of its rare mistake – a temporal relaxation of its guard – which enabled Digital Equipment Corporation (DEC) to slip into the market with its mini-computers. For the first time, IBM faced a troublesome competitor in the office market.

Sun Tzu has given the following elaboration:

> *The one who is first to occupy the battlefield to await the enemy will be fresh and at ease; he who comes later to rush into the fight will be exhausted. Therefore, the skilful general imposes his will on the enemy by making the enemy come to him instead of being brought to the enemy.*

Gillette is another good example of keeping with this passage. Although Wilkingson Sword's introduction of the stainless blade in the 1960s, and the bonded blade (a metal blade fused to plastic) in 1970, stunned Gillette, it was able to catch up with its own Trac II, the world's first double-bladed razor. This was followed six years later by Altra, the first adjustable double-blade razor, and many other improvements since. And because Gillette was astute enough to be watching Bic which was preparing to introduce its own use-and-throw razor, Gillette hit the market first with the Good News disposable razor. Although Good News production cost is higher while margin is lower when compared with other Gillette products, it has effectively blocked Bic from taking control of the disposable razor market. As a result, Gillette market share is indisputably the largest with some 65 per cent. In sacrificing short-term profits, it has protected its market share. If Gillette had adopted a "wait-and-see" stance, Bic could most likely end up dominating the disposable segment which represents some 40 percent of the razor blade market, and thus considerably undermining Gillette's position.

Similarly, if you should suffer a sudden price attack from one of your competitors, this is what Sun Tzu suggests:

> *Should someone ask: "If attacked by a large and orderly force, what shall I do?" I reply: "seize something that the enemy holds dearly so that he has no choice but to yield to your will".*

A good example is the response of the American tire manufacturer, Goodyear, when its French rival, Michelin, tried to enter the American market with its new radial tire technology in the early 1970s. Not only did Goodyear improved its own technology but it further counter-attacked in the European market which is Michelin's home turf. When Michelin cut prices by 5 per cent in Europe in a bid to throw off Goodyear, the latter cut 15 per cent. Michelin was thus forced to concede the American market to protect its traditional territory.

And, be wary of the "wait-and-see" attitude. If you have been well informed about your competitor, then you should know to what extent and for how long he is able to finance the price war that he has embarked against you. You should also find out where he is weak so that you could direct a counter-attack. I know a manufacturer who was once threatened by a rival when the latter secured a bank loan which he used to finance an aggressive price war against his products. The manufacturer had a rumor out that his rival was financially over-stretched and abusing the conditions of the loan. He then got his high-placed friends in the bank's head-office to act on that rumor to recall the loan. *Result:* the price war was extinguished before it can do much damage.

OVERT OFFENSIVE STRATEGY

This is open warfare where you publicly flex your muscles and launch into a "straight-for-the-throat" attack against your competitor. For this activity, Sun Tzu has given some good advice. Offensive action can come in two forms. First, to knock out a business rival so as to take over his company, e.g. takeover bids. Second, to knock out a competing product so as to take over its market share. In looking at the first case, let us take note of Sun Tzu's advice:

> *Generally in war, the best policy is to take the enemy's country whole and intact; to ruin it is not so good. Also it is better to capture the enemy's army than to destroy it; to take intact a regiment, a company or a five-man squad is better than to destroy them.*

Indeed it would serve no purpose to be destructive. Can you imagine a corporate raider using tactics which would mortally damage the company he wishes to take over? What is the point of having control of a company whose management and staff are badly demoralized, whose financial resources exhausted, and image and credibility have already been ruined?

And when you have successfully taken over the company you have bid for, remember this advice from Sun Tzu:

> *Be kind towards captives, and care for them. This is called "using the captured foe to strengthen one's own force".*

It is often the case that the moment one company takes over another, the victor would send in its own management team to relieve the one in the vanquished firm. Sometimes only the chief executive in the vanquished firm would be replaced while the other managers would be allowed to remain albeit under "watch" for a while before they are also sent packing. This is really a waste of human resource. If one has been well-informed about the company he is trying to take over, he should also know the capability of each of the key managers in the company. Thus, after he has taken over the firm, he should see to it that the capable people are not only retained but are further assured of employment and fair treatment. Instead of questioning the loyalty of the employees in the firm that has been taken over, remember they are like employees anywhere in seeking job security and willing to work for whoever is fair to them.

Caring for the people in a vanquished State is so important that Sun Tzu has made another observation:

> *To win battles and make conquests and take over all the subjects but failing to rebuild or restore the welfare of what he gains would be a bad sign, so called "wasteful stay".*

Therefore, do not make yours a "wasteful stay" for otherwise there is not much point in fighting in the first place.

As for inroading a competitor's market share, such offensive warfare is mainly based on superiority in numbers which has been most explicitly explained by Sun Tzu as follows:

By discovering my enemy's dispositions and at the same time concealing mine from him, I can concentrate my forces while he must divide his. Knowing his dispositions, I can use my total strength against a part of his. If he is ignorant of mine, he will have to spread out his force to defend every point. This will give me superiority in numbers.

The idea here is to concentrate one's forces. This is based on the fact that when one tries to fight on too wide a territory with too broad a range of products, the probability of his success is greatly decreased. Such a move would cause him to over-spread his resources. Going on this principle, one should therefore concentrate on what he is best at doing, and keeping as close as possible to a single product until it is strongly positioned. By attacking on a narrow front, resources are thus concentrated and not spreaded too thin.

Federal Express has learned this lesson. Its "hub-and-spoke" concept – all packages come to a central hub in Memphis to be sorted and re-routed via an outbound flight instead of from point to point – gave it the competitive edge over other courier companies. But by trying to compete with air freight forwarders like Emery and Airborne with three classes of service – priority one (overnight), priority two (2-day delivery), and priority three (3-day delivery) – Federal Express started losing money. It then concentrated on just priority one – the reason why people use couriers – and began to do all right.

Domino's Pizza has also learned a good lesson on the need to concentrate one's forces. Its founder, Thomas S. Monaghan tried at first to do both "eat-in" and home delivery. In realizing subsequently that doing both was one too many things to implement and control, he focused instead on just home delivery. Today, Domino's Pizza is the most successful home delivery business in the American fast-food industry.

161

In keeping your forces concentrated, avoid taking on more than one competitor at a time. This was the mistake which Royal Crown made in the 1960s. Although it caught both Coca-Cola and Pepsi-Cola off-guard with its Diet Rite Cola, it failed to concentrate its resources on this winner in the diet soft drink segment which represented almost 50 percent of Royal Crown's earnings. By continuing to field a full line of colas against Coca-Cola and Pepsi-Cola, Royal Crown found its resources were insufficient to match the combined resources of the two giants. The profits from Coke and Pepsi were used to finance their own diet cola brands (Tab and Diet Pepsi) which eventually reduced Diet Rite with its three years' headstart into near obscurity.

Since colas are discussed, we might as well look at Coca-Cola's biggest mistake. As the first on the scene, it has been entrenched as number 1. But over the years, it has been making the mistake of not concentrating its forces, in terms of products and marketing theme and thence is finding its market being eroded. Product-wise, we now have New Coke, Classic Coke, Diet, Cherry, Diet Cherry, Caffeine-Free and Diet Caffeine-Free. It can be quite mind-boggling making a choice so much so I often end up simply asking for a Pepsi, or if my wife is around, a Diet Pepsi. In the case of marketing theme, Coca-Cola is forever changing its theme when compared with Pepsi Cola's youth-oriented "Come alive, you're in the Pepsi generation" which has remained fairly consistent the past 27 years. Over the years, Coca-Cola has toyed with "It's the real thing"; "Coke adds life"; "Have a Coke and a smile"; "We have a taste for you"; "The Real Choice"; "Coke is it"; "Catch the wave"; "Red, white, and you"; "You can't beat the feeling"; etc., while Pepsi's theme has steadily taken root among its young drinkers.

While concentrating your force, remember to keep something in reserve. This is what Sun Tzu must have meant when he says:

*If double his [the enemy's] strength, divide our force
into two to use as "alternate strategy"..*

Therefore, when on the offensive, even if you have plenty of funds, do not spend all at once. Spend only what is necessary to "keep the enemy on the move" as Sun Tzu has put it. Keep the rest in reserve to be used, should the competitor launch a counter-attack.

Superiority in numbers tends to place the odds in favour of the larger companies. This is because the larger company can always afford a bigger advertising budget, employ more capable scientists to develop its R&D effort, hire more salesmen to push its products, etc. But Sun Tzu has also warned about relying too much on superiority in numbers:

In battle, having more soldiers will not necessarily give victory. Never advance by relying blindly on the strength of military power. It is sufficient to concentrate our strength, estimate the enemy's position and seek his capture. But anyone who treats the enemy with contempt and disdain will only end up being captured.

From this, we see that there can also be weakness in strength. Take for example, the illustration of the imaginary Warrior Electronic Company we have read earlier in Chapter 5. As the firm grows, it is inevitable that more and more employees will have to be hired. Most of these employees (staff) will be providing services for others (line) and thence will never be involved in actual production or get to meet customers. Decisions in such companies may take weeks or even months as compared to a smaller firm where the entrepreneur-boss may take only a few minutes to decide since he does not have to seek the approval of others. A small company may thus be able to surprise a big company with a new product.

McDonald's may enjoy superiority in numbers but Burger King found a way to overcome this in the early 1970s. The assembly-line system gives McDonald's its strength in uniformity of its hamburgers – e.g. the Big Mac is standardized "two all-beef patties, cheese, lettuce, onions, pickles, and special sauce in a sesame seed bun – which allows instant delivery at low cost". Hence, when Burger King came up with the "Have it your way, with or without pickles, etc." strategy, McDonald's was stumped. It could not tamper with its finely-tuned system just to match Burger King's promise.

To knock out a competitor's products so as to dominate the market share, one must be quick in creating or seizing opportunities. As Sun Tzu has said:

> *The one who is first to occupy the battlefield to await the enemy will be fresh and at ease; he who comes later to rush into the fight will be exhausted.*

In this respect, let us learn from Paul Fireman, a camping equipment distributor who went to an international trade fair in 1979 and saw the Reebok custom track shoes. After buying the U.S. license from the British manufacturer, he not only made and sold US$1.5 million of shoes in 1981, but was also quick to see the running fad had peaked. While Nike continued to make running shoes which piled up in its warehouses, Fireman switched to introducing the Reebok "Freestyle" which is a flamboyantly-colored soft-leather aerobic shoe, in 1982. Spurred by the encouraging response of both aerobic-dance instructors and students, Reebok successfully expanded into tennis shoes, basketball shoes, walking shoes, and even children's shoes (called "Weeboks") as well as a "Cross Trainers" for those who want an all-purpose shoes. Fireman's foresight for market segmentation has enlarged Reebok's market share today to become a billion-dollar business.

In taking the offensive trail, one should try to avoid repeating mistakes for as Sun Tzu suggests:

The skilful general does not require a second levy of conscripts nor more than one provisioning.

and,

He [a skilful fighter] wins by making no mistake. Making no mistake means already having established the certainty of victory: conquering an enemy who is already defeated.

It is not only costly to keep on making mistakes, but you are also alerting your competitor of your intention. Besides, it will not do any good to the confidence and morale of your staff. When Seven-Up positioned its lemon-lime drink in 1968 as the non-cola, i.e. the alternative to Coke and Pepsi, sales in its first year went up 15 per cent. But ten years later, under a new management and flushed with financing, Seven-Up went on an advertising campaign of songs and dances. This was a mistake – singing and dancing have been the established strengths of Coke and Pepsi. That year, it was the only one of the top 10 soft drinks in the USA to lose sales.

The next mistake was the refusal of Seven-Up's management to go on a non-caffeine campaign (to show its difference from Coke or Pepsi which contains caffeine). In 1982, forced by declining sales, Seven-Up took up the non-caffeine trail. It then made the mistake of splitting its concentration by launching Like, a decaffeinated cola, which confused its consumers. Moreover, although the non-caffeine campaign pushed it to third place from fourth in the soft drinks industry, Seven-Up's concentration in the campaign faltered when it went on to include the non-artificial colors' declaration. The latter inclusion was a flop because many established products are known to use artificial colors and no one is complaining. Seven-Up not only made many mistakes but had confused its own ranks instead of those of its competitors.

Sun Tzu has also made the following calls:

> *They [the soldiers of a skilful general] carry war materials from the homeland but forage on the enemy. Thus, the army is plentifully provided with food.*

and,

> *Hence, the wise general sees to it that his troops feed on the enemy.*

and also,

> *When we are deep in enemy's territory, become the guest of the enemy.*

The term, "enemy" should not be taken literarily to refer just to competitors but should also include those we seek to ally with. Thus, when my business manager presented her marketing plan to promote business at the Cili Padi Thai restaurant at The Mall shopping complex, her proposals were almost faultless. She suggested making the Thai restaurant more exciting for its patrons by redecorating the restaurant to give it a more authentic "Thai" look and flying in native Thai cultural dancers and traditional musicians to stage daily performances. As Malaysia's premier and most expensive Thai restaurant, it was also suggested that the restaurant should offer more than fine and exotic dining. If we also set up a few "sampans" against a giant wall mural depicting the Bangkok "floating market" as backdrop, and have native Thai craftsmen demonstrating vegetable-carving, flower-plaiting, umbrella-painting, etc., on these "sampans", we would not only provide cultural glimpses but also create an ambience befitting the premier Thai restaurant in the country.

She had even worked out the operational details and costs which was why I said the report was almost faultless. Considering the restaurant had since its opening been in the red, I told my business manager that her report was incomplete. She was baffled and protested: "But I have covered the objective, what we should do, how to go about doing those things, and even worked out the cost involved. So what's wrong?"

What was wrong was the lack of thought given to who should be footing the cost! It was on account of the above sayings by Sun Tzu that in the end we not only did not have to pay a single cent but we managed to make some money from the promotion (this did not include the subsequent increased business revenue). We managed to convince the Tourism Authority of Thailand (they were well-funded and active then in their "Visit Thailand" campaigns) that they will get more mileage from supporting our promotion than if they were to carry on putting up billboards all over Malaysia and on the back of buses. Thai International Airway and Carlsberg Brewery were also roped in to contribute to the promotion.

Sometimes one can also "feed on the enemy" by riding on their successes or publicity. These are usually the smaller firms which are able to find a segment of the larger and more established market yet small enough for them to develop and at the same time defend. A good example is Computervision which has made good in the wake of IBM by making computer-aided design (CAD) computers. By concentrating on a niche or segment of the market, i.e. CAD computers, Computervision has entrenched itself against the industry leader, IBM.

COVERT OFFENSIVE STRATEGY

In using covert offensive strategy, one tries to keep as low a profile as possible while making his offensive moves. In staying out of the limelight, his moves are virtually unknown to the world at large. This is what Sun Tzu says:

> *Fighting to win one hundred victories in one*
> *hundred battles is not the supreme skill. To break*
> *the enemy's resistance without fighting is the*
> *supreme skill.*

One man in the Asian business world who is a master strategist albeit a relatively unknown one, was my former employer, Mr Robert Kuok. Unlike Chrysler's chairman, Lee Iacocca whose achievements have been widely publicized, very little is known about the way of the Asian "sugar king". In the mid-1980s, he was one of those behind the purchase of Central Sugar Refinery (CSR) in Malaysia from the Malayan United Industries (MUI) group. While MUI retains five percent equity, the balance was shared between the Malaysian Government-backed Pernas group and Morgan Grenfell, one of the big securities' brokers who, only much later was confirmed to be acting on behalf of Mr Kuok when one of his top aides was appointed managing director of CSR. By this move, he quietly and substantially enlarged his share of the Malaysian sugar market.

Keeping a low profile while making offensive moves would surely be in line with Sun Tzu's treatise on the use of deception:

> *All warfare is based on deception. Therefore, when*
> *capable, pretend to be incapable; when active, inac-*
> *tive; when near, make the enemy believe that you*
> *are far away; when far away, that you are near.*

In the early 1980s, when people called Nestle, a "sleeping giant", its president, Helmut O. Maucher, happily said: "I hope our competitors believed we are still sleepy". And no wonder, for in 1984, the "sleeping giant" suddenly woke up hungry and went on a gobbling spree in the United States, swallowing an assortment of companies which included contact-lens maker, Coopervision, Hill Bros. Coffee and the cosmetic division of Warner Communication.

Similarly, the virtually covert exercise of enlarging the little holes in monosodium glutamate bottles from 1 mm to 1.5 mm by some Japanese manufacturers, reflects Sun Tzu's call to "break the enemy's resistance without fighting". Who could have imagined that this quiet move to enlarge the bottles' holes would result in consumers unwittingly putting more MSG in their food? It is said that consumption (and thus, sales) of MSG went up by 50 per cent. And not even a word of protest from the consumers or health-protection groups since everything was done so subtly.

Sun Tzu goes on to say:

> *Thus, the general skilled in war places priority in attacking the enemy's strategy; next best is to disrupt any alliances of the enemy; to be followed by confrontation of his army.*

As mentioned earlier, this was what Burger King did to McDonald's when introducing the "Have it your way, with or without pickles, etc." promise in the early 1970s. This threw a spanner in the programmed assembly-line production system which has been McDonald's strategy in churning out standardized hamburgers fast and cheap.

Sun Tzu advises:

> *Whenever the enemy presents an opportunity, take it quickly. Anticipate him by seizing what he holds dear, checks the situation of his force, and secretly launch the attack. Therefore, at the start of the battle, be as coy as a maiden; when the enemy lowers his guard and offers an opening, rush in like a hare out of its cage and the enemy will be unable to defend.*

When Pepsi-sponsored megastar, Michael Jackson was in Bangkok in August 1993 to kick off his world tour, he postponed his concerts twice, citing acute dehydration caused by the heat and humidity. The Coca-Cola Company promptly carried out a half-page advertisement in the English-language dailies, The Nation and The Bangkok Post, with the message: "Dehydrated? ...There's Always Coke, and a picture of an inviting chilled bottle of Coca-Cola. This is truly a case of speedily seizing an opportunity to get at the enemy!

Hence, be reminded against making the mistake of taking a "wait-and-see" attitude. In the modern business world, if one is slow to act when the opportunity presents itself, there may never be a second chance. In 1978, the American battery manufacturer, Duracell, which is the world's leading producer of alkaline-manganese batteries, "invaded" the British market from its plant in Belgium. Duracell rapidly gained market share as it was unopposed by the British giant, Ever Ready Limited which decided in the following year to continue with its zinc carbon production against the development of its own alkaline-manganese battery. Falling profitability from a declining market grew to crisis proportions until the company eventually decided to bring out its own alkaline-manganese battery which it launched in 1983 – some five years behind Duracell!

SUMMARY

Several strategies are discussed in this chapter. They have been categorized under three main groups – defensive strategy, overtly offensive strategy, and covertly offensive strategy. Their choice depends on whether: it is worthwhile to fight; one is strong enough to fight; one is yet weak in defence even though he may be strong enough to fight; and it is a situation with no option. Hence, executives are exhorted to take their responsibility to their organizations seriously and temper their natural aggression. At the same time, one is taught to take every advantage of opportunities and to be wary of threats so that one can be adept in the Art of War and make the best of the situation.

In defensive warfare, rather than merely taking a passive acceptance of one's position in the face of stronger rivals, seek the offensive with the clear objective of protecting one's market share. Sometimes leading companies will also take a defensive stance to protect what they have got. Never assume we will never be attacked but to prepare against such. Defensive strategy is thus more proactive than reactive. The lesson is that one should be disciplined in seeking to consolidate one's strengths. Such could involve chopping off products which are not doing well or replacing those which are about to enter the decline phase as depicted on the product life cycle. At the same time, one should monitor the competitors' movement. Should we suffer a sudden price attack, be wary of the "wait-and-see" approach. If we have been well informed about our competitor, then we should know the extent of his financial capability and where are his weak points which we could launch a counter-attack.

In overt offensive strategy, i.e. open warfare where one publicly flexes muscles and launch into a "straight-for-the-throat" attack against the competitor, it serve no purpose to be destructive. This is because there is no point in taking control of a company whose management and staff are demoralized, whose financial resources are exhausted, and image and credibility are ruined. And when taking over the company bid for, do not waste the human resource. Be well-informed about the company that is being taken over so that we know the capability of each key manager in the company and retain the capable ones who should be assured of employment and fair treatment. Offensive warfare is mainly based on superiority in numbers whereby one's forces should be concentrated. This means not fighting on too wide a territory with too broad a range of products to avoid over-spreading resources. In keeping your forces concentrated, avoid taking on more than one competitor at a time. While concentrating your force, remember to keep something in reserve. Therefore, when on the offensive, even if you have plenty of funds, do not spend all at once.

While superiority in numbers tends to place the odds in the larger companies' favor because the larger firm has larger budget to advertise, hire the best or more staff, do not over-rely on such as there can also be weakness in strength. Larger companies take longer time to make decisions when compared with a smaller firm. A small company may thus be able to surprise a big company with a new product. Sometimes one can also "feed on the enemy" (this include those we allied with, e.g. joint ventures) by riding on their successes or publicity.

Using covert offensive strategy requires one to keep as low a profile as possible while making his offensive moves. In staying out of the limelight, his moves are virtually unknown to the world at large. Quietly he shall attack his rival's strategy and prevents his alliance with other competitors. And when a competitor presents an opportunity, do not hesitate to seize it because if one is slow to act, there may never be a second chance.

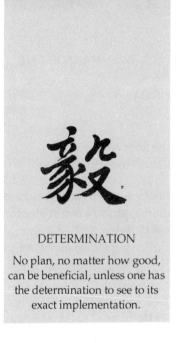

DETERMINATION

No plan, no matter how good,
can be beneficial, unless one has
the determination to see to its
exact implementation.

CHAPTER 12
Strategy Implementation

HAVING GONE OVER strategy formulation, the next stage is to look at how the chosen strategies can be implemented to give the desired results. Here, I would like to clarify that I shall be departing from the Western approach towards strategy implementation which tends to address topics such as organizational structure, organizational design, organizational behavior, management selection and development, management information systems and communications, since I have already discussed them albeit briefly.

Instead, to demonstrate how the selected strategies can be implemented effectively, I shall take the unorthodox approach of relating this activity to some of Sun Tzu's principles which can be grouped under each of the following areas of study:

1. use of deception;
2. secrecy;
3. flexibility;
4. speed and timing; and
5. use of direct and indirect methods.

Each of these areas is essential towards realizing the goals which an organization aspires to attain and for which strategies have been developed in the first place if an organization were to cope in the increasingly competitive arena of the external business environment.

USE OF DECEPTION

Deception has been in use in various forms since time immemorial and it is a reality of business just as of war. Since I too have resorted to the use of deception in my time (and I may yet have to use it sometime in the future), it is no good my taking a hypocritical stance of advising you against using it as a way of doing business. Some things in life are just inevitable.

Let me cite this simple incident as an example: A major tenant stormed into my office one day when my secretary was out and complained that the receptionist made him sit for 10 minutes before letting him in to see me. Claiming she was rude to him, he demanded her immediate punishment or he would forget all that we had earlier discussed at his office for a second shop at The Mall. My mind raced through these facts:

1. This guy was well-known as a self-important character and it would take an extremely patient person not to be rude to his bullying and pushy ways (sometimes I even feel like wriggling his neck);
2. The said receptionist in fact was a most courteous and dedicated staff;

3. He rarely visits his existing shop which was managed by one of his employees, and thus, the receptionist may not have recognized him;
4. The receptionist did not let him in because I was on the line with my boss; and
5. I nonetheless need him to open the second shop.

Seeing how angry he was, and realizing the truth of the saying – "truth is not what I told you; truth is what you chose to believe" – I decided to placate him by conforming to his state. In his presence, I intercommed the office administrator and growled: "I understand the receptionist has been rude to one of our best customers. This sort of thing shouldn't be allowed. Send someone to replace her now and get her to your room for an investigation. I want a report by today!" That action satisfied the old man and when he left my office about 15 minutes later, I had his signed agreement. The moment he left, I beelined to the office administrator's office and found him busily interviewing the receptionist. Wearing my grim-faced mask, I asked what happened. After hearing out the receptionist, I allowed my face to relax a little and smiled at her, saying: "Okay, I believe what you said. That man can be quite irritating. But do remember, a receptionist's job is never an easy one. So always try your best to be patient, even with such irritating blighters. We'll let this drop". While the office administrator looked relieved that no tedious paper work was in store for him, the girl looked as though she could hug and kiss me.

Everything as you can see from this incident was an attempt to deceive. I had no intention to punish the receptionist. My action was calculated to please the tenant and at the same time get the receptionist away from the reception desk so that on his way out, they would not have to meet and possibly get into another incident (the tenant is quite likely to gloat and taunt her). At the same time, the deception also worked to remind the receptionist that:

1. Failure to do a good job will not be tolerated; and
2. The management is nonetheless fair and just, with the result that she felt even more grateful for having her explanation accepted and the case dropped.

Hence, in some ways, the use of deception to manage incident such as this one can be helpful towards attaining the company's goals. In this case, a business deal was concluded and staff morale improved by the knowledge that the management would be firm yet fair.

This is only a simple illustration of deception. In the cut-and-thrust of the business world, more can be involved. As Sun Tzu has observed:

> *All warfare is based on deception. Therefore, when capable, pretend to be incapable; when active, inactive; when near, make the enemy believe that you are far away; when far away, that you are near. Hold out baits to lure the enemy; feign disorder and strike him. When he has the advantageous position, prepare against him; when he is strong, avoid him. If he is prone to choleric temper, irritate him. Pretend weakness so that he may become arrogant. If he is at ease, put him under a strain to wear him down. When his forces are united, divide them. Attack where he is unprepared; appear where you are not expected.*

As we can see above, holding out baits is a common method of deception. By this move, one can bring the enemy to where one wants to fight, or in the modern context, bring the customer to where we want him to spend his money:

> *Thus, adopt an indirect route and divert the enemy by enticing him with a bait.*

This is what most businessmen have done to divert shoppers from patronizing their competitors. You would have been familiar by now with the various sales gimmicks like, "Hurry! Clearance Sales – Only While Stocks Last", "Mystery Gifts For

First 300 Shoppers", "Congratulations, You Have Been Selected To Participate In Our Lucky Draw To Win A Free Trip To Paris", etc. These baits have been most successfully used to lure and entice shoppers. In the supermarket war, the use of some items as "loss-leaders" – selected consumer items which are deliberately sold below cost – to attract shoppers is nothing new. I was once invited to join an exclusive club which was prepared to waive its entrance fees because its membership committee has considered my case thoroughly and found I make a desirable member. Flattered as I was, I declined. A year later, I heard one of my staff complaining the club had subtly increased its annual fee. It seems she too was invited to join on the same terms as I was offered.

Another suggestion which Sun Tzu has put forth, is:

> *Therefore the skilful commander imposes his will on the enemy by making the enemy come to him instead of being brought to the enemy. To do this, he offers the enemy some advantages...*

As I was told by a businessman who supplied tanks to a regional armed force: "I sold my tanks very cheap... you can say, at an almost give-away price... But my contract stipulated sole right to supply the ammunition and to provide maintenance and repair service. Naturally, ammunition and spare parts prices are very much marked up. While you would hear deafening shots each time they fire during gunnery practice, I hear pleasant cash-register's tinkling". Such two-part pricing or complementary pricing is common in the computer market: hardware may come cheap but software is a different matter altogether...

Other methods of deception include fakery and the creation of illusions. In the first instance, fakery may occur when one pretends to be humble, weak and sometimes, even feigning stupidity. Such pretences are calculated to play up the enemy's ego, encourage his arrogance and thus deceive him into a false sense of security so as to extract information out of him or to trap him. I had a very good teacher in my late father who would, when the occasion demanded, clown around and play the fool until those who did business with him were lulled into a false sense of security that they would readily divulge information to him or close the deal with my father, believing they had the advantage since they were dealing with a "fool".

As for the creation of illusions, the objective is to confuse the enemy about your true intention. Thus, the one who creates the illusions will become unpredictable in the eyes of the enemy who will then be in no position to judge the situation. If you are skilled in creating illusions, then each time your enemy meets with you, he will have to incur both time and resources to do a new and thorough assessment of you.

However, do watch out for deception by others:

> Do not pursue an enemy who pretends to flee... Do not swallow baits put out by the enemy.

What you can do to others, they too can do to you. Learn early then that nothing is for free and it is greed that will lead one to his ultimate downfall. I once very nearly fell for an offer to buy into a company whose accountant had very cleverly window-dressed the books of accounts. It was an art of illusion which despite my diploma in accounting and finance, very nearly taken me in. Luckily, my wife's nagging based on her "womanly intuition" dissuaded me from buying into that company which folded a few months later.

SECRECY

It is vital that no one (this includes both friends and foes) should know your plan unless it suit your purpose to let them know. There is a very simple explanation for this secrecy because as Sun Tzu has observed:

> By discovering my enemy's dispositions and at the same time concealing mine from him, I can concentrate my forces while he must divide his forces.

Knowing his dispositions, I can use my total strength against a part of his. If he is ignorant of mine, he will have to spread out his forces to defend every point. This will give me superiority in numbers. And if I were to use my superior strength to attack an inferior one, those I deal with will be in dire straits. The enemy must not know where I intend to attack. For if he knows not, he must prepare for possible attack in many places; and in such preparation, his forces shall be so spread out that those I have to fight at any given point will be few.

This passage is so clear that I need not elaborate further. Instead, I shall move on to show you what Sun Tzu has advocated in terms of secrecy:

Do not let your enemy understand the plans concerning your troops movement.

and also,

He [the general] changes his arrangements and alters his plans so that no one knows what he is up to.

I must caution though that secrecy should not be allowed to become an obsession. I know quite a number of managers who are so obsessed to the extent of regarding even petty issues as secret that they could not bring themselves to delegate tasks since such would entail divulging information to those who had been delegated to perform the tasks. One of them dare not even entrust his secretary to type confidential memos to his boss, insisting she bring in the typewriter for him to type out the memo himself. As professionals, we must be able to judge what information is confidential and to what degree so as to determine who could have access to the information.

FLEXIBILITY

Very early in this book, I have touched on the need to be flexible and not rely on the one-best way of doing things (see Contingency Approach in Chapter 1). Sun Tzu has this to say:

> *When I win a victory, I do not repeat the tactics but respond to circumstances in limitless ways...Thus, the one who can modify his tactics according to the enemy situation shall be victorious and may be called the divine commander.*

If you keep repeating your tactics, your enemy can easily predict your move. I once saw a man playing poker. He was the most predictable player I have ever seen. He would doggedly follow to the end whenever the good cards came into his hands, or would be among the first to throw in when he held bad cards. It would have helped if he had called bluff sometimes but he fixedly followed his pattern. Result: he was the only loser that night because everyone could predict his cards.

Sun Tzu observes that:

> *Conformation of the terrain is the soldier's best ally...*

I believe this is in line with what modern marketing books have called the "marketing concept" which simply means finding out what the customer needs and then working on satisfying such needs for a profit. This is in contrast to the traditional production view of "producing what one is good at making and then trying to sell it". British manufacturers have been criticized for their slowness to change to the marketing concept. When my wife and I visited Iona Island, off the south-western Scottish coast, we stayed at the island's Abbey where the meals served were mainly vegetarian fare. Yearning for meat, I visited one of the island's restaurants one evening and ordered lamb chops. As I missed fried eggs,

I requested the waitress for two fried eggs to come with my chops. She looked lost for a moment, said she got to check with the chef, came back after a few minutes to say: "Sorry, we only serve what is indicated on our menu". If that restaurant has been managed by a marketing-orientated restauranteur, I could have my eggs or anything I fancy albeit I would have to pay a high price in order to satisfy my fancy.

At this point, it is important to point out that a strategy can be viewed as a coherent direction whereby to further the marketing function. Hence, even though such direction should ideally remain unchanged once a strategy has been selected, one can still change if the original strategy is found to be unworkable. This is because the struggle for supremacy in the business "battlefield" can often be fierce and risky. One must always be flexible and know when to fight and when not to:

> *When our casualties increase, then withdraw. If our force is so much weaker than our enemy's, we should avoid him; for if a small army is stubborn, it will only end up being captured by the larger enemy force.*

As the adage goes: "He who runs away lives to fight another day". One survives by being prudent rather than being stubborn. The ability to manage change and to ensure continuity through a period of change is becoming more and more vital for success. Thus, a company may have invested heftily in a project that its management is unwilling to face reality when the investment is unsuccessful. Believing it has invested too much to quit, the company may carry on throwing in good money even after the venture has turned bad. In such cases, it may be necessary to divest (thus cutting losses) the unsuccessful project and re-invest the proceeds elsewhere rather than stubbornly clinging on to it and sinking deeper into the red.

SPEED AND TIMING

As we have already learned very early in this book, Sun Tzu has emphasized planning because he was able to see that prolonged warfare carries no benefit. According to him:

If victory is long delayed, weapons are blunted and the ardor of the soldiers will be dampened.

Thus, the strategy we adopt must be carefully thought out so as to provide for a quick victory. Also remember that strategy shall remain a mere theory unless it is implemented, i.e. acted on. Hence, once a decision is made as to what strategy shall be adopted, we must not allow any unnecessary delay in its implementation. As Sun Tzu says:

Speed is the essence of war.

Delays or hesitancy will only allow our competitors to get wise to our strategy. Such knowledge will also enable them to make preparations to counter our proposed move. Bristol-Myers had learned the importance of timing and the consequence of alerting the enemy. In June 1975, it introduced Datril which has the same pain-relieving potent and safety as Johnson & Johnson's Tylenol. The only difference is that Datril has been priced a dollar less than Tylenol. But Bristol-Myers made the mistake of market-testing Datril which alerted Johnson & Johnson into action. Two weeks before the scheduled Datril advertising campaign, Johnson & Johnson notified (as proprietary practice) Bristol-Myers of its intention to match Datril's price. This alarmed Bristol-Myers into moving forward its television commercials which led Johnson & Johnson to complain to the Council of Better Business Bureaus, networks, and the Proprietary Association. The Datril advertising plan was disrupted when the networks required copy changes and CBS and NBC refused to run the Datril spots. As a result, Datril failed to achieve more than 1 per cent of the market share.

If Bristol-Myers had more confidence in its product and timed its launch without carrying out the market-test, it could have achieved different results. Hence, as Sun Tzu has so wisely written some 2,500 years ago:

> The well-timed swoop of a hawk enables it to strike its prey. Therefore, the momentum of one who is skilled in war will be overwhelming and his decision to strike must be well-timed.

Remember earlier when I wrote about how it took Ever Ready Limited five years to respond to Duracell's alkaline-manganese battery? Who says there is little to learn from history?

USE OF DIRECT AND INDIRECT METHODS

In Chapter 1, when I told you to go by the "systems approach", I made a reference to the following Sun Tzu's passage:

> In battle, there are only the direct and indirect methods of fighting but they give an endless combination of maneuvers. For both forces are interlocked and using one will lead to the other; it is like moving in a circle – you can never come to an end. Who can determine when one ends and the other begins?

From this passage, we find that Sun Tzu recognizes the need to use both methods in waging war. Through the interchangeable deployment of these methods, one can always keep the enemy in doubt as to one's real intention and at the same time enabling one to secure victory. And as I have also told you about the "contingency approach", do bear in mind that one ought to be highly flexible when using both methods interchangeably. This means one must provide for situations where the enemy does not respond as anticipated. Hence, either method must be capable of replacing the other at any time. Let us see what Sun Tzu has said about using these methods:

> *Generally, in battle, use direct methods to engage the enemy's forces; indirect methods are however needed to secure victory.*

As a simple illustration, if I were to submit a written proposal to a business party and subsequently meet with him to persuade him to act on my proposal, this would be the direct method. At the same time, if I know anyone who is close to him and who can influence his decision, then any action on my part to harness the support of the said third-party to influence and wrap up the deal would be the indirect method. Such actions (in harnessing support) can include making some gestures – appropriate or inappropriate (e.g. bribery) ones – for the purpose of obligating the third party in some way that he will be willing to exert his influence on my behalf.

Although inappropriate gesture such as bribery is regarded as unethical (and also highly illegal in some countries where there are strict laws against this practice), it is nonetheless being practised and used as a competitive tool by many businessmen to secure a contract, etc. I have heard the art of bribery has become so refined that one particular businessman who resorted to such practices no longer gives an outright bribe in money or in kind. Instead he would invite the person he wishes to bribe, to a poker game, where despite holding good cards, he will happily throw in his hand and lets the other person win. The winner is also happy that the businessman is saving his "face" by not offering money outright but making the gesture of letting him win money in a "fair" game.

The following gestures had helped in my career-development todate:

1. *Doing Something For The Kids* – When I was managing The Mall, I learned that one of my business associates had a 5-year-old son who would go "ga-ga" over the characters out of television's cartoon series, "Teenage Mutant Ninja Turtles". When The Mall brought in the costumed characters as part of the complex's promotion, I remembered this little fact and arranged for the little boy to attend the Ninja Turtles' party where he not only danced with "Michaelangelo" but also had a photograph taken with all four turtles. Nothing inappropriate about my gesture but the youngster's father has never ceased to appreciate what I had done.

2. *Let People Off The Hook* – When the purchasing officer of a soft-drink manufacturer telephoned me in 1986 to say: "Khoo, I have miscalculated my sugar stocks and production needs. Although I have signed an order with you for 120 tons yesterday, I hope you will, as a favor, without mentioning to my boss, allow me to rescind the contract and issue you another for 50 tons instead?" Despite knowing my own boss would be extremely displeased with the reduced sales, I unhesitatingly said that would be no problem. The following month, the purchasing officer pushed an extra 200 tons (I believe it was at a rival refinery's expense) my way.

It is not difficult to understand then why Sun Tzu has written:

Winners are those who know the art of direct and indirect strategies.

One must simply work harder (and of course, smarter) at being creative. For example, when I was used as a "football", that is, when I approached Mr X for assistance in resolving a problem, he very helpfully referred me to Mr Y, who was as helpful in referring me to Mr Z, who in turn was certainly most helpful in referring me back to Mr X. Ah, you got the picture!

Well, I listened to good old Sun Tzu and decided on using both the direct and indirect approaches: I invited all three parties for lunch (without each of them knowing the others were invited) and when we were happily seated together enjoying our sharksfin soup, I asked most innocently: "Well, you remember I was talking the other day about Project Lido ... er, which one of you, by the way, can give me the 'green light' to proceed?"

As Mr X could have no more excuse to make references since everyone concerned was present and he was not prepared to risk losing my goodwill then, I got one problem off my chest that day.

There are endless applications in store. And nothing is more essential than an appreciation of the need to use both direct and indirect methods in their interchangeable forms for success. Take the view then that one must not be confined to only one particular course of action. Instead, identify various options and use them according to the needs of the situation.

SUMMARY

This chapter looks at how the chosen strategies can be implemented to give the desired results. Instead of taking the Western approach towards strategy implementation which tends to address topics such as organizational structure, organizational design, organizational behavior, management selection and development, management information systems and communications, the unorthodox approach shows implementation from the point of usage of deception; secrecy; flexibility; speed and timing; and usage of direct and indirect methods.

Each of these areas is necessary if an organization were to realize the goals for which strategies are developed in the first place to enable it to cope in the increasingly competitive arena of the greater business.

Deception which is used today as it was during Sun Tzu's time and earlier, is seen as a reality of business just as of war. Deception commonly takes the form of the holding out of baits, such as when one lures the customer to where one wants him to spend his money. Businessmen have, through various sales gimmicks like clearance sales, free gifts, contests, loss-leaders, waiving entrance fee, etc., diverted business away from their competitors in this manner. Other methods of deception include fakery, i.e. where one is seen to be humble, weak, or even stupid when he is not, and the creation of illusions, in order to become unpredictable in the eyes of the enemy who will then be incapable of judging the situation accurately. In attempting to deceive others, one must also watch out for deception by others since two can play the same game.

Secrecy in business is necessary to ensure that no one know one's plan unless it suit one's purpose to let them know. One should however not become obsessed with secrecy to the extent of regarding even petty issues as secret and thus impairing one's delegation effort since effective delegation would entail divulging information to those who had been so delegated. As professionals, we must be able to judge what information is confidential and to what degree so as to determine who could have access to the information.

Flexibility is needed to prevent the enemy from easily predicting one's move. Flexibility will also enable one to effectively apply the marketing concept which simply means finding out what the customer needs and then working on satisfying such needs for a profit. While a strategy can be viewed as a coherent direction whereby to further the marketing function, it should still be subject to review and change if found to be unworkable. The ability to manage change and to ensure continuity through a period of change is becoming more and more vital for success.

Speed and timing are also necessary because as Sun Tzu has emphasized, prolonged warfare carries no benefit. It is important then that the strategy we adopt must be carefully thought out so as to provide for a quick victory. The same goes for deciding on the strategy to adopt as well as its subsequent implementation. Delays or hesitancy will only allow our competitors to get wise to our strategy. Such knowledge will also enable them to make preparations to counter our proposed move.

Sun Tzu has further recognized that both direct and indirect methods must be used in waging war. Through the interchangeable deployment of these methods, one can always keep the enemy in doubt as to one's real intention and at the same time enabling one to secure victory. This is in line with the 'contingency approach', and the earlier call for flexibility. In short, one must provide for situations where the enemy does not respond as anticipated. Hence, either method must be capable of replacing the other at any time. In making formal (i.e. direct) approaches, businessmen often resorted to indirect methods, such as making some gestures – appropriate or inappropriate ones – for the purpose of obligating some third party in some way that he will be willing to exert his influence on my behalf. Inappropriate (and illegal in some countries) gestures include bribery and corruption while more appropriate ones may take the form of harnessing the support of mutual friends, doing favors for the person we are dealing with, e.g. doing something for his kids or helping to make his work easier at some time or other when we are in a stronger bargaining position. As the applications are endless, it is essential that one appreciates the need to use both direct and indirect methods in their interchangeable forms for success. One must not be confined to only one particular course of action and instead should identify various options and use them according to the needs of the situation.

PART V

Conclusion

ADAPT

This character emphasizes the
need to be flexible for as Sun Tzu
urged: "Confrontation of the
terrain is the soldier's best ally
in battle" meaning that one
must adapt to one's situation
or circumstances.

CHAPTER 13

Evolution of Management Theories and The Japanese Appreciation of Sun Tzu's *Art Of War*

SINCE THE INDUSTRIAL Revolution, organizations have grown in numbers and in size, and accordingly have become more complex, ambiguous and paradoxical. In seeking to improve our understanding of human activity in organization, both managerial practitioners and academics representing a wide range of disciplines began to develop theories about organizational behavior during the early and middle part of the twentieth century.

Each of these theories come with inherent strengths and weaknesses and can be applied to one organization or the other but NOT all organizations. For example, the mechanistic approaches to organizations found in the classical organization theory of Henri Fayol and developed by Frederick Taylor's scientific management, excel in stable environment where method and cost efficiency is required in churning out standard products in precise and orderly manner. But the mechanistic organization will be vulnerable in the face of changing circumstances where emphasis is shifted to flexibility and creativity. The human relations school has also found disparity in the treatment of organizational members in that the structured organizations tend to impose an alienating and dehumanizing effect upon employees, especially those at the lower levels of the organizational hierarchy.

Up to the 1960s most studies on organization searched for the "one best way" of organizing. But this approach was never fruitful since there is no one best way of organizing. Instead, Burns and Stalker, while looking into the possibility of identifying a continuum of organizational forms ranging from mechanistic to organismic, found that successful adaptation of organization to environment depends on top management's ability to interpret the conditions facing the firm in an appropriate manner and to adopt relevant courses of action. In her study, Joan Woodward found that successful organizations match structure and technology. Both studies show that the organizing process involves choices dependent on achieving a balance or compatibility between strategy, structure, technology, the commitment and needs of people, and the external environment. This contingency theory was subsequently driven home by Lawrence and Lorsch, both of whom concluded that what matters is not the existence of particular management style or organization structure but that the organization characteristics of the company fit into the environment in which it operates.

In short, it is possible to blend various theories to match the internal organization structure and processes with its external environment. Management must therefore be concerned with achieving "good fits".

THE APPLICABILITY OF THE *ART OF WAR* AND THE CHINESE NEGLIGENCE

This "good fits" concept exactly reflects Sun Tzu's sentiments when he wrote the *Art of War* some 2,500 years ago. We have further seen in this study how Sun Tzu's ideas can find ready application in today's management. It is indeed a great loss for the Chinese that, like Sun Tzu's successors in the ancient State of Wu, they have not been able to appreciate this treasure inherited in Sun Tzu's work, the *Art of War*. If the Chinese have not neglected this treasure trove, they need not have to suffer criticisms of their management skills. As John Fukuda has observed in his book, *Japanese Style Management Transferred*, Chinese managers are not exactly renowned for their management skills.

On the other hand, the Japanese, especially the larger corporations have made it a point to study Sun Tzu's work, especially in his call to be flexible. They have accordingly achieved "good fits" by blending the Western organization theories with some modifications suitable to the task or environment in which they are operating.

THE JAPANESE RESPONSE

Before World War Two, Japan copied its corporate system from the West. Japanese companies were run much like most Western companies after the Industrial Revolution. In copying the Western organization concept which is modelled after the military, the Japanese took only the form while the substance remained Japanese, or communal. This is a hint of the Japanese nature – eager and curious to learn from others, not embarrassed to copy their ideas, but highly innovative in modifying what they have copied to suit their needs.

Two articles in the *Harvard Business Review (1981)* have argued that the Japanese "miracle" rests primarily on well thought out and rigorously applied methods of production management. The principles, it is argued, are no different from those regularly practised in the USA 25 years ago: "...what we in the West have forgotten or let slip, Japanese management has taken up and perfected".

THE JAPANESE RESPONSE TO THE CLASSICAL ORGANIZATION THEORY

Interest with problems of practical management have led classical theorists like Fayol, Mooney, and Urwick to codify their experiences of successful organization for others to follow. Taking the stance that management is a process of planning, organization, command, coordination, and control, they have also propounded that organizations could be managed more efficiently if certain universal principles were applied.

Some of these principles are widely followed in Japanese organizations while others are totally ignored. To be fair to the Japanese, some of the principles were already used by them well before the writings of the classical theorists came about although the approach or terminology may differ.

Take for example, the classical principle of "discipline" which was inspired by Western military dictates, seeking obedience, application, energy, behavior, and outward marks of respect in accordance with agreed rules and customs (Does this not remind you of Sun Tzu). The Japanese, with their own military legacy, views this principle as *bushido*, that is, the way of the warrior. *Bushido* is their own code of conduct which resembles European chilvary but much more narrow in that it is confined to the relations between the *samurai* (warriors). By this code, a *samurai* is expected to give his unswerving loyalty to his lord and to obey him without question, even to die for him if called upon to do so. Most modern-day Japanese are brought up from young on tales of valor of the old-day *samurai* which explains why loyalty, submissiveness and deference to authority are given such high value by both Japanese employers and employees.

The code of *bushido* also enhances the classical principle of "unity of command" because it dictates that no samurai could serve more than one lord. Hence, "discipline" and "unity of command" as advocated by the classical theorists need no modification as they are useful in reinforcing the Japanese own heritage of hierarchy in their organizations. Other classical principles readily accepted by the Japanese without modification are "centralization (of authority)", *espirit de corps*, and to some extent, the "scalar chain" principle.

Japanese society was traditionally feudal in nature with divisions into four main classes: *samurai*, peasants, artisans and merchants. Within the *samurai* class, there were numerous sub-divisions ranging from the *daimyo* (lord) to the *ashigaru* (foot-soldiers). Centralization of authority would thus rest on the *daimyo* over his particular fief or province, who in turn, with other *daimyo* would come under the *shogun* (overlord). Although the Meiji Restoration in 1868 abolished the class system, the system of organization in Japan today is still somewhat feudal rather than modern.

There is some modification however in the application of the "scalar chain" principle. Although hierarchy in a Japanese corporation is as much a system of mutual service as one of top-down control, the use of organization charts is quite non-existent. Kenichi Ohmae has written in his book, *The Mind of the Strategist*, that most Japanese organizations lack even a reasonable approximation of an organization chart. An example is the automobile manufacturer, Honda. With annual turnover of US$5 billion, it is obviously quite a flexible, strategy-oriented company, capable of making prompt and far-reaching decisions. But nobody knows how the firm is organized since all of its employees are lumped together as "automobile assembly workers". This is where the modification appears: although top Japanese executives retain a strong hold on authority in the hierarchical control, they have deliberately played it down so as to leave room to blend with the organismic approaches to organization for the purpose of facilitating communications and flexibility.

But this does not mean that Japanese corporations are without red tape and ritualism. Japanese industry depicts organizations which are, in some respects, highly authoritarian and in their demand for rigorous conformity, highly bureaucratic. However, this has come within the sphere of what Max Weber has called the rational form of organization which is the more positive side of bureaucracy, given the practices of appointment by qualification and a continuous striving for efficiency.

The Japanese have however kept a wide berth from the classical principle of "division of work". While Japanese organizations do have functional departments, e.g. production, marketing, personnel, etc., task specialization is temporal being subject to a job-rotation system which by mutual understanding allows a worker to switch around. There is a link here to the traditional farming village lifestyle where every member of the village is equal and a generalist. Besides, tenured employment in allowing a worker to learn a broader range of skills during his career through job-rotation (thus enhancing his value and contribution to his organization) has worked so well for the Japanese that they are reluctant to introduce anything which will drastically affect their system.

Before 1949, Taylor's scientific management gained an immediate and impressive foothold in Japan and influenced management thinking for generations after the translation of *Principles of Scientific Management* (published in the USA in

1911) into the Japanese language. This favorable reception could be attributed to the fear then in Japan of strong labor-management conflict, a perception of inefficient business and government practices relating to imperial conflict, the establishment of the *zaibatsu* (the influential Japanese industrial groups), and a pressing need to reform personnel practices.

However, scientific management was subsequently rejected by the Japanese in the 1950s. An increasingly educated workforce had by then read and believed the American literature which said the old ways would result in growing disinterest, low commitment, decrease in efficiency, increase in defects, higher employee turnover and absenteeism. This has found support in Kiyoshi Suzaki's book, *The New Manufacturing Challenge*, where he observes that quality problems, machine breakdowns, and frequent schedule changes tend to disrupt the Japanese efforts to develop a smooth material flow on the production floor. Besides, rigid job descriptions restricting areas of responsibility – the Taylorist approach – also hamper the coordination of the total production system. Hence, he suggests developing manufacturing flexibility to expand operators' skills and to fully utilize their collective skills and experience to counter the traditional Taylorist approach.

THE JAPANESE RESPONSE TO THE HUMAN RELATIONS SCHOOL

The human relations school which had its origin in the Hawthorne experiments started out on the narrow Taylorist perspective of investigating the relation between conditions of work, and the incidence of fatigue and boredom among employees. As the research progressed, the focus shifted to many other aspects of the work situation, such as the attitudes and preoccupations of employees and factors in the social environment outside work.

Given that Japanese management was very much influenced by American ideas after the War, and as the human relations movement was at its zenith in the USA at that time, it is not surprising that this theory has found much acceptance in Japan. As both Mayo's social view of man and the later view of the self-actualizing man propounded by Maslow, Herzberg, McGregor, etc., met with the Japanese way of thinking, they were very well received.

As we have learned earlier, to the Japanese businessman, organization really means people. Hence, to a Japanese manager, the welfare of employees take priority over profits. Unlike their Western counterparts, Japanese corporate presidents pay greater attention to employees than to shareholders (i.e. the owners). The Japanese approach which attempts to hire young employees and keep them on until mandatory retirement means that employees very often spend their entire working life in the same company. They cannot leave the company even if they do not like it unless they are prepared to risk their security. Shareholders are however free to sell their stocks anytime they wish. Both management and workers are thus committed to work together in the interest of the organization (i.e. the people in it) and not for the owners. Organizations provide a web of relationships with peers, subordinates, and seniors which are acknowledged as important. This is the social view which Mayo has conceived: the desire to stand well with one's fellows, the role of sentiments, and the instincts of human association.

The importance and effects of groups and group behavior, particularly the findings of Roethlisberger and Dickson on how workers can restrict output and penalize those who failed to conform with group norms, reflects Japanese work groups' behavior today. As Professor Masakazu Yamazaki of Osaka University notes, one of the reasons that Japanese workers are more interested in their work group is that they hold on to their group relations for individual support rather than rely on abstract ideological beliefs for individual support. In this way, tasks are assigned to work groups, not individuals, and the group collectively accepts responsibility for the achievement of targets. Owing to the central importance of group efforts in their thinking, the Japanese are extremely sensitive to and concerned about group interactions and relationships.

In this spirit, an employee who has been handed a certain responsibility will not limit himself to this responsibility alone but will further interpret his duty as it affects his group. The group attitude is closely analogous to that of Western marital relationship whereby the Japanese workers recognize problems and concerns in work relations as they focus on building trust, sharing and commitment. Each worker believes that his personal fortune and those of his colleagues will rise or fall with that of the company and seeks a more sensible consensus to get along well with one another to further the company's long-term well-being. This has indirectly led to the harmonization of the workplace. Although conflict exists as in any Western organizations, it is kept to a relative low level. Hence, managers and workers are seen wearing the same uniforms, eating in the same canteen and communicating on a lateral level allowing for a bottom-up consensus-type decision-making process.

In this condition, the Japanese were primed to receive the concept of quality control circles (QCC) which were introduced to Japan in 1950 as a result of a series of lectures on statistical quality control by Dr. William Deming and in 1954 when the US Department of Defence invited Dr. J. Juran, a noted quality control expert to Japan to help Japanese firms win procurement orders from the American military. The Japanese were then seeking to improve production techniques and productivity by integrating worker values into the organization. The Japanese industry was rapidly transforming into higher technology areas requiring more sophisticated work skills and was finding it difficult to recruit and keep employees in traditional job categories.

From Dr. Deming and Dr. Juran, they learned to reverse the traditional American 85-15 formula, i.e. placing 85 per cent of the responsibility for quality control on line managers and engineering staff, and only 15 per cent on plant workers. As Dr. Juran argues, quality control must become an integral part of the total production process. Thereafter, the Japanese systematically exposed all hierarchical levels – from shopfloor workers to top management – to statistical quality control techniques with continuous training and discussion being the norm and thus escalating the QCC movement.

Observe then how the Japanese strategic effort at developing employee responsibility and job enlargement has an impact on the structure and climate of the total organization. Trust is regarded here as essential, and both managers and foremen are trained to accept individual worker responsibility. As Mr. Hiroshi Takeuchi, a prominent Japanese author and advisor to Nikkeiren (Labour Questions Research Committee) writes: "An organization that trusts its employees and entrusts work to them has no need for supervisors". This may be the essence of McGregor's Theory Y wherein managers assume that such things as the capacity for shouldering responsibility, the potential for development, and the readiness to direct behavior toward organizational goals are all present in people but again you can find similarity to the remarks of Sun Tzu.

In Japanese business organizations, the principle of equality is used to remunerate employees. The principle of equality means that all newly recruited workers, white-collar or blue-collar, shall start work on the same level of pay. A few poor performers would get less in annual increments but those few with exceptionally high ratings will not get extra than the masses. However, this does not mean the Japanese do not seek to motivate their employees. Maslow would be pleased that the Japanese do see each individual as having economic, social, psychological and spiritual needs, and Japanese executives believe it is only when such needs are well met within the organization's sub-culture that employees can largely be freed for productive work. But they are primarily concerned with groups of people and not so much with individuals. Thus, the principle of equality prevails: there can be no heroes and elite employees. And since everyone has equal opportunity, through the job rotation system, everyone knows that he will have the chance to move between functions, offices, and geographical locations.

THE JAPANESE RESPONSE TO SYSTEMS THEORY

The first attempt to integrate some of the diverse elements was by a group of researchers from the Tavistock Institute of Human Relations who adopted a socio-technical systems approach. The term "socio-technical" was coined by social scientists to describe the linkages between the software and hardware aspects of management-worker relationship in organizations. The software/hardware analogy with computers is intentional to emphasize their interdependence rather than their separate impact in relationship. The hardware metaphor refers to the technology while management software can be defined as the system of rules, regulations and standard operating procedures governing work, tasks and human behavior.

This belief of human behavior occurring within a socio-technical system is clearly reflected in the Japanese organizations described so far. Japan with its pluralistic society has developed work systems which combined human intellectual effort with machine precision and computational facility in a way unrivalled by Western societies. It is neither hardware nor software alone, but the combination of both!

SUMMING UP

Like the West, Japan has its fair share of organization failures side by side with the success stories. After all, I have only reviewed those literature which looks at the larger and more established Japanese organizations. Nonetheless, the principle holds. Those unsuccessful cases are characterized by management's poor judgement and leadership, hostile management-worker relations, stagnant organizations, poor human resource development, defective financing policies, inability to match technological change, inappropriate cost management, all of which reflect an inability to adapt and achieve the "good fits".

But where those successful Japanese organizations are concerned, they have shown through their organic evolutions, that they can change the way they are. Once they have identified the conditions on which their organizations are dependent, they can look towards blending the organization theories for optimum effectiveness.

To drive this point home, it is interesting to note that the typical Japanese firm operating overseas employs an approach to management distinctively different from the typical host country firm. Take the USA, for example, where the Japanese firms would modify their management to suit the needs of the United States rather than to replicate the form developed in their native Japan. Nonetheless, they still retain a good deal of Japanese style and remain quite distinct from most American firms. This, if I may say so, is largely due to the ability of the Japanese to adapt to circumstances and also their strategic outlook, both of which have been developed over time as a result of the foresight to appreciate, as well as the willingness to seek and apply the knowledge found in Sun Tzu's work, *Art of War*.

Index

SEMINARS

Many executives and organizations have attended Khoo Kheng-Hor's seminars which range from a one-day or one-and-a-half-day "Management, the Sun Tzu Way" program to a two-day seminar cum workshop, or short three-hour to three-and-a-half-hour talks in various applications of Sun Tzu's *Art of War* to specific areas such as Management and Leadership, Marketing Strategies, Human Resource Management, Customer Service Management, Team-Building, etc.

WHAT THEY SAY:

"We have all been buffeted the last 30 to 40 years by ideas and concepts of management from the famous schools of business in England and the United States, and all of a sudden, we have in our own backyard, principles and management practices which are very similar." – **K.B. LOW, Managing Director, IBM Singapore**

"If a seminar is a form of drama, Mr Khoo has definitely displayed excellent showmanship." – **The Management Development Institute of Singapore**

"After hearing Mr Khoo's talk, I decided that my executives must also hear him talk." – **GAN THIAN LEONG, CEO, Brunsfield Group of Companies, Malaysia**

"You brought to life the concept first written 2,500 years ago. Your real life executive experiences are both vivid and current." – **PAUL CHAN, former Director & General Manager, Hewlett-Packard Singapore (Sales) Pte Ltd**

"On behalf of the Polytechnic, I would like to thank you for your excellent presentation during last Saturday's seminar. It was well received, with many chief executive officers and senior executives finding the seminar interesting and enlightening. It was also an eye-opener for those who were hearing Sun Tzu's strategies and philosophies for the first time." – **BRUCE POH, Director of International Development and Industry Services, Nanyang Polytechnic, Singapore**

"We received very good feedback on the talk. Mr Khoo captivated the participants with his tongue-in-cheek style of delivery." – **Singapore Institute of Insurance**

If you're interested in engaging the Author to speak, please contact:

Stirling Training & Management Consultants Pte Ltd
128A Tanjong Pagar Road, Singapore 088535
Fax: 02-5357265